KATHARINA VON DER LEYEN

77
DATES
WITH YOUR
DOG

KATHARINA VON DER LEYEN

77 DATES WITH YOUR DOG

teNeues

CONTENTS

Introduction

Why we have dogs? 8

Chapters

1 Make jokes! 12

2 Visit a zoo together 13

3 Can you dig it? 14

4 Break bread with the hungry 15

5 The wisdom of water 16

6 Turn your ho-hum walks into adventures 17

7 Pat, touch, feel 18

8 Let your dog take the lead! 19

9 Immortalize your dog in pictures 21

10 Jackpot for your dog 22

11 Dive deep 24

12 Don't talk so much 26

13 Cook for your dog! 28

14 Mail call! 30

15 Doggie Love Nibbles 31

16 Swimming lessons for dogs 32

17 Build a sandbox 35

18 Mental communication (just shut up for a while) 36

19 Row, row, row your boat 39

20 Find your keys 40

21 Make your dog ice cream 42

22 Make your dog a cloth rope toy 44

23 Praise your dog for once!
   (The best exercise of all) 45

24 Have a picnic 46

25 Change the mood 48

26 The right balance 51

27 Take a siesta together 52

28 Bring me a tissue! 53

29 To conquer the heart of your dearest dog once and for all:
   Mayday Liver Toffees 54

30 Nerve food for dogs 56

31 Try clicker training 58

32 Discovery trail 60

33 Jump on a trampoline 62

34 Take a beach vacation 63

35 A mixtape for your dog 64

36 Train an emergency whistle signal 66

37 Get in the pool 71

38 Play hide-and-seek 72

39 Happy Birthday 74

40 He relaxes on command! 76

CONTENTS

41 Teach a shy dog how to play 77

42 Write your dog a letter 79

43 Make yourself and your dog useful 80

44 Show your dog that kids are
terrific playmates 82

45 Wag more, bark less – dogs as philosophers 83

46 Turn your living room into a doggie gym 84

47 Making trades 85

48 Dig for treasure together 87

49 Taking a hike 88

50 Let your "only dog" go for a walk with
a dog walker 89

51 Listen to your gut 91

52 For short-haired dogs: Wipe them with a dry washcloth 92

53 For longer-haired dogs: Hair slides 93

54 Become a positive thinker 93

55 Make a conscious effort to walk slowly 95

56 Take a page out of your dog's book:
Let the past go 96

57 Cooking for everyone! Chicken and pearl barley soup for
you and your dog 98

58 Work out with your dog/Dog Walk Fitness 100

59 Tell your dog a story 103

60 "Go to bed" 104

61 Break up with your boyfriend or girlfriend
   if he/she doesn't like your dog 107

62 Travel companion 108

63 A build-it-yourself bottle game for dogs 110

64 Thank your dog for eternal life 112

65 Just be together and do nothing for a change 114

66 A scavenger hunt for your dog and his (and your!) friends 116

67 Take extra good care of your senior dog 118

68 Liverwurst tea 121

69 Share a smoothie with your dog 122

70 Make a scent pillow for your dog 124

71 Plant a fruit crate with grass 127

72 Go for a walk in the hours before dawn 128

73 Go to a major dog show
   with your dog 130

74 Lay down a trail 133

75 Walking in the snow 134

76 Grain-free Christmas Liver Biscotti 136

77 Embarking on the final adventure 138

Biography 140

WHY WE HAVE DOGS?

Every relationship eventually succumbs to a certain routine. It's no different with our dogs, our oft-cited best friends. You always take the same path through the same park, so sure, you can call your girlfriend on your cell while you walk. Or you take the stroller along and squeeze in a quick walk between errands. You put down a dish of dog food while your own scrambled eggs are cooking on the stove, and you give him a quick scritch while you're watching TV or on the phone.

And suddenly you realize that the dog is just sort of "in tow." Because he's a dog, he does it without complaining – maybe he's not quite as obedient as usual, or he doesn't come over and cuddle quite as much. Of course, compromise is part of life. As is hurrying. But pay attention to how often your dog becomes just another detail – probably too often.

Carve out time that is just for you and your dog. No matter how much we love them, our time is often what our dogs don't get heaps and heaps of.

Relationships are all about bonds: an invisible link from one party to the other that lets us feel what the other one is feeling, that makes us sit up and take notice when something is off with our partner. But when we only engage with others (whether canine, avian, or human) on a superficial level, it's easier to miss the quieter subtle signals. As for me, I have eight dogs (I'm not really quite sure how that happened anymore), and my favorite thing to do is be a giant goofball with them. The rest of your life is so very serious, and dogs are happiness personified – you have to take advantage of it. The more silly stuff I do with my dogs, the more they pay attention to me, the better they obey, and the less I have to correct them. It's because we have a strong relationship, and they are only too happy to follow my lead.

Once a day, concentrate your full attention on your dog for a set period – even if it's just ten minutes. Run across a meadow just with him. Spend ten minutes focusing only on stroking, scritching, and petting your dog – without skimming through a magazine. Feel him: the thickness of his ears, the warmth of his paws, feel his ribs and his muscles. Sing to him while you walk him (assuming you are somewhat musical – otherwise you might have to spend a very long time looking for your dog!). Don't just go for a walk, pick out a specific grassy strip and hide little hot dog pieces in it. Mess around in the dirt until he comes over on his own to see what the heck you're up to.

Completing a route together is not what makes a relationship. It's about spending time together. That's why I have written a list of 77 dates you can or should make with your dog – as a kind of starting gun. Once you've really gotten into the groove, you'll probably think of many more things to do on your own. Make sure that the bond connecting you and your dog is thick, strong, and indestructible.

After all, isn't that why we have dogs in the first place?

With warmest wishes, Katharina von der Leyen

I

MAKE JOKES!

Unlike people, nearly all dogs have a sense of humor. That's why they are so easy to get along with. So we humans have to make ourselves bearable for our dogs, too. Most of us are just way too serious in general. Dogs can't understand that because they fundamentally believe that every day is a gift. They don't really have bad moods.

So before your dog gives up on you and becomes just as dull as most of his colleagues and their dull, dull owners, rediscover your inner clown! Just let it go and be silly! Do ridiculous things! Tickle your dog's feet,

make fun of him, and run behind him before quickly turning and letting him chase you the other way. No one will thank you more for it than your dog. And, I promise, no one will think you are less crazy than your dog. He'll be relieved because you have finally figured out how to deal with life's vagaries.

2

VISIT A ZOO TOGETHER

There are still zoos, wolf sanctuaries, and wildlife parks that don't mind you bringing your four-legged friend along. Usually dogs are not allowed in elephant, predator, or monkey houses, but there is plenty to discover and sniff outside as well. Will your dog stay cool as a cucumber when he sees a gorilla? What will he say to the noises that sea lions make? What does he think of bison? And what will he do when he hears the howling of his cousins, the wolves?

A trip to the zoo is fun for the dog and the human when you go together!

3

CAN YOU DIG IT?

Dogs love it when we take part in their hobbies. And most dogs love to dig. So jump in and dig with them! If you're lucky enough to have a yard or live on the beach, start digging a hole using just your hands until your dog – who has no doubt grown curious to see what cool thing you are doing – comes over and joins in. If you want to dig in a park or forest, make sure you stay away from paths or open areas, because a person (or dog) could easily step in your hole and be injured. But digging off the path and away from tree roots is totally okay!

Take along a stick to bury to make the whole thing even more exciting. It's important that the digging is a shared activity and your dog doesn't completely take over (it's about that team feeling!). If he digs enthusiastically, watch him for a while, then move him over a little and take a turn digging in his hole before you let your dog dig some more. It's up to you how long you continue the game. If you see a bunch of Peruvians coming toward you, you'll know you've arrived on the other side of the world.

4

BREAK BREAD WITH THE HUNGRY

Eating together is an extremely social act: that's why we invite friends over for dinner, and that's why families try to eat at least one meal together every day. It's no different with our dogs – but because we worry about teaching them to beg if we give them something from our plates, we leave it alone, and we eat separately.

Surprise your dog: sit down with him in a park, on a bench in the city, by the lake, wherever you want, and unpack a nice turkey or roast beef sandwich you've brought along (vegetarian options are okay too!), and share it with your dog. Each of you gets half. Make a ritual out of it – every Thursday you eat a hot dog together on the riverbank, for example. Or on your patio. Your dog will jump for joy!

5

THE WISDOM OF WATER

If you're not afraid of getting wet, water is a lot of fun, and not just for dogs. The next time you walk with your dog along a creek or around a lake, jump in with your dog! Jump around, splash your dog with your hands, run through the water — and enjoy the amazed look: What now? We're just getting wet to be silly? *Just because?*

6

TURN YOUR HO-HUM WALKS
INTO ADVENTURES

Walking the same few routes day in and day out can get a little old for everyone concerned after a while. Turn the daily chore into a memorable event!

While your dog is busy sniffing something important, silently drop a few choice treats on the edge of the sidewalk and get very interested in that area and the grass growing there until your dog gets curious and comes to see what you are doing.
At the next corner, hide a toy in much the same way: don't say anything, but fumble around in that area until he comes up of his own accord and looks to see what you're up to. Or "accidentally" drop your keys or gloves and send your dog back to get them.

You'll see: Instead of a monotonous trot around the block, you can easily turn your normal route into an exciting excursion.

7

PAT, TOUCH, FEEL

Adults tend to always pet their dogs the same way, according to their inner motto, "We've always done it this way, and it always worked just fine." As I already mentioned under "make time": try petting your dog with your eyes closed, or while wearing a blindfold, without letting yourself be distracted by anything else.

Feel his coat, how dense his hair is, the little hairless places, how soft his skin is, how thick his ears. Trace the bones of his skull, how much space there is between his eyes, and run your finger down his nose. Slowly stroke your dog with a flat hand and make long, slow movements along his fur (not against it): across his shoulders, his breastbone, his tummy, along his legs. Try to feel his elbows and knee joints; move your hand down his legs and carefully touch the tendons between his hock and his rear paw. Massage his skin in gentle clockwise circles. When your dog is so relaxed that his breathing sounds like he's fallen into a coma, gently run your fingers over his paws, carefully feel his toes and paw pads, and carefully

feel in between the pads. Feel each individual vertebra in his tail and try to count them.

When you're done, you'll see your dog through new eyes – and he will adore you for the incredible massage.

8

LET YOUR DOG TAKE THE LEAD!

Assuming you don't *already* let your dog drag you this way and that, wherever his nose might lead him, through the great outdoors on your walks, you should occasionally give your dog the opportunity to literally take the lead. Hook your dog up to a ten-foot line and head out, and when you get to an appropriate place – a meadow, a park, a beach, a vacant lot (a forest is not so good because you don't want to scare any wildlife that might be in the underbrush) – let your dog go where he wants to go. Just follow him, and when he sniffs one spot for a long time, take your time and observe him. Some dogs have to practice this because they are so used to doing what their master wants. The expression that comes over these dogs' faces when they understand that they are the ones calling the shots is priceless: some dogs literally crease their brows when they see that the usual roles are now reversed.

By the way, this is also a useful exercise if you ever get lost: when you explain to your dog (who is now used to leading the way) that you want to go home – he'll probably get you on the right track. Or he'll take you to the nearest supermarket, and that's quite useful too!

9

IMMORTALIZE YOUR DOG IN PICTURES

In the modern smartphone era, we are constantly snapping pictures of every-thing that crosses our screens. Unfortunately, we hardly ever sort these pictures, and once they land on our computer, we rarely look at them again.

They're much too precious to be ignored like that! Take all of those won-derful snapshots of your dogs and make books out of them (there are many providers on the Internet who will take your photos and make small or large photo books, posters, photo puzzles, memory games, etc.).

And even better: In the age of social media, it isn't hard to find good, professional dog photographers, sketch artists, and painters. Give yourself the gift of a truly wonderful portrait of your truly wonderful dog – one that reflects and records his personality (and maybe your sense of humor as well) for posterity. American photographer Amanda Jones, for example, published a book with portraits of the same dog taken over roughly 12 years – as a newborn or puppy and then later, with a gray muzzle and the wisdom of age in his eyes. Pictures like that are more than snapshots; they are wonderful, happy, and somewhat bittersweet memories. A few of my dogs are here in this book as well.

Special dogs deserve special memories, don't you think?

10

JACKPOT FOR YOUR DOG

Special treats are an excellent way to motivate your dog when you want to teach him something new, or when you want him to do something that really goes against his nature – that's when you give him a jackpot. For work that goes above and beyond, don't even consider giving him dry dog food – that's minimum wage stuff. For example, if you teach him a special whistle to call him away from chasing a wild animal (or something else really exciting – one dog's bunny rabbit is another's cyclist or jogger), that demands a truly extraordinary reward.

Pay attention to the foods your dog is prepared to sell his soul for. Many dogs are prepared to work miracles for rotisserie chicken. Meatloaf is also amazing. You can also check the meat counter or butcher for inexpensive ends and leftover bits of cold cuts, sausage, meatloaf, and roast pork that are not attractive enough for humans to eat, but are perfectly tasty, fatty, and wonderful for dogs. A lightly spiced organic liverwurst can also move mountains if you put it in a food tube and squeeze out small portions for the dog to lick off when he has excelled. You can buy inexpensive food tubes on the Internet that are dishwasher safe and reusable. Cream cheese is also a hit, as is a mash of tuna or salmon and cream cheese – also squeezed out of a food tube.

Dried fish or freeze-dried beef is also very effective. Some dogs love pizza crust – try it!

The important thing is that you save these rewards and offer them only for Olympic-level talents and tasks your dog performs. If you give a jackpot in passing or just because your dog is cute, you are ruining its value!

II

DIVE DEEP

Sometimes a dog needs a real challenge. Today, his search for food is ridiculously easy thanks to our modern standard of living. Why not spice it up a little? Fill various bowls with water – one bowl with only two inches or so, one with a little more, and so on. Throw a few hot dog pieces in the first bowl, an anchovy in another one, some pepperoni in a third one – you can use as many bowls as you want, but it is often more fun if there aren't too many bowls. One Labrador we know drank the entire bowl of water just to get at the anchovy!

But this "experiment" is definitely fun for both parties, there are funny reactions: one spaniel tried to splash the fish out of the bowl with his

paws. My sneaker-sized mutt Barthl makes short work of this task: on his first try, he tried to get in the bowl and tumped it over. Then he lay down happily in the puddle and ate the anchovy. Now he knows how to do it. Okay, I should probably mention that this game should not be played in your living room. It is the canine equivalent of a really wet sandbox and a three-year-old. Although, come to think of it, you could do that with your dog too ...

If you don't want to set up a bunch of bowls, you could also use a kiddie swimming pool that's not filled up too much – unless you have a dog that likes to dive and blow bubbles underwater. Those dogs are out there too.

12

DON'T TALK SO MUCH

People rely on words. As a result, we tend to spew text at our dogs: We hold long monologues and say things like "I've told you that 1000 times!" and "Do you HAVE to do that?" as though our words had any meaning to our dogs.

But they don't. Our words mean absolutely nothing to them. They can learn to differentiate the sound of individual words (Australian Shepherd Chaser, who belongs to American psychologist John Pilley, can match 1,022 words to the correct objects thanks to a special training method), but if you say to them, "Oh, sweet baby, you are the very, very best dog ever," that says bupkis to them. Zip. No more than "Blah, blah blah blah, blahblahblah-blahblahblahblahblah, blahblahblah." So if your dog still wags his tail happily and smiles back, it's because your body language is saying what you mean: you think your dog rocks. The set of your shoulders tells him more than a thousand words.

It is precisely the people who talk incessantly to their dogs who make it hard for them to understand or even hear their commands because they tend to get lost in a sea of words. To the dog, it all sounds like babbling – some with more emphasis, some with less.

The more you talk to your dog, the less he listens to you, because your comments all run together into a kind of background noise (you see this sometimes with old married couples: the husband always says "Yes, dear" and "Mm-hmm" at regular intervals without registering a single word of what his wife has just told him).

Try it yourself: for one week, only tell your dog the most necessary things and concentrate more on your body language. Pay attention to what your body is saying to your dog, how much tension you are conveying to him, whether your shoulders are actually pointing in the direction you want him to go, and whether you might accidentally be blocking the car door with your body even though you are telling him to jump inside.

You'll see: your dog will suddenly pay more attention to you because he can't always rely on being able to hear you. If you only say what is truly important, these words will have a greater impact. And if you don't call him before you turn a corner, but just go where you want, he will automatically pay better attention to make sure you don't go out of sight.

13

COOK FOR YOUR DOG!

Sometimes you should give your dog something special to eat. Especially if your dog is a frustrated hunter, this recipe for Doggie Meatloaf should be an excellent consolation prize! The loaf is delicious and smells heavenly too. It also keeps for a while in the refrigerator, so you can give it as much as your dog needs each day.

Ingredients:
· 8 oz chicken liver
· 1 pound ground beef
· 4 cups grated potatoes
· 1 cup grated carrots
· 2 eggs
· ½ cup rolled oats
· 1 teaspoon parsley, finely chopped

Preparation:

Preheat oven to 350°F.

Boil the chicken livers in water for three minutes, then pour off the water and chop up the liver.

Put the ground beef in a large bowl and combine with the potatoes, carrots, and the chopped liver.

In a small bowl, beat the eggs and mix in the oats and parsley.

Pour the contents of the small bowl into the large bowl and knead the mixture with your hands until it forms a ball.

Put the ball into a greased pan and bake on the middle rack of your oven for 90 minutes at 350°F.

When done, remove from the pan immediately and allow to cool for 20 minutes (under close supervision – put the loaf up high or in the fridge if necessary!) before cutting. Will keep in the refrigerator for about a week.

14

MAIL CALL!

On rainy days, or if you have an older dog, or a dog who hasn't learned (yet) how to play, it's important to come up with some interesting things for them to do.

Make a package for your dog! Get a box and some old paper and wrap up squeaky toys, yummies, little chew bones, individual dog bone treats, a beat-up favorite toy, a piece of pepperoni, a ball, etc.

Close up the package – you can use the lid if you have a shoebox, or lay a piece of cardboard or newspaper over the top – and present your dog with his package. If you use a ribbon and a bow it should be easy to undo. Let him unpack everything and rejoice right along with him!

15

DOGGIE LOVE NIBBLES

You can observe "nibbling" among dogs who like each other very, very much: with pursed lips, they will gently nibble on each other – the same move they make when they are looking for a flea in their own fur. If your dog is feeling mellow and flops on his back to encourage you to be silly, run your fingers through his coat and very, very gently lift bits of skin between two fingers. But be careful that you don't accidentally pinch him! Most dogs love it. But if your dog turns away to show you he doesn't like it, you need to respect that.

If your dog likes to give you doggie love nibbles, it's best if you wear a sweater or a long-sleeve shirt so this display of affection doesn't hurt.

16

SWIMMING LESSONS FOR DOGS

Not every dog takes to the water like a duck, but you should encourage him to swim because it has all sorts of physical benefits for both man and his best friend. However, simply chucking your dog into the water is a) rude, b) rarely helpful in actually achieving the desired result, and c) can actually traumatize him.

Sometimes, just seeing his human happily jump into the water and start swimming will get the dog to join in. However, many dogs will stay on shore, complaining and howling because his human is voluntarily putting himself in such peril, but remain determined not to abandon the safety of dry land. But even these cases can be helped.

It makes things easier for both man and dog if the air and water are at a comfortable temperature. Wear a bathing suit or shorts and a T-shirt, and put Crocs or Birkenstocks on your feet so you don't have rocks poking your bare feet the whole time. If your dog really doesn't like the water, he should wear a snug-fitting harness or a doggie life jacket so you can stabilize him without having to grab his fur.

Go with him on a loose leash into the water. Start out with very shallow water so that your dog first learns that water is fun, you won't leave him, and no monsters will jump out at him. Keep a good hold on your dog as you go into deeper waters. He needs room, about an arm's length, to move his paws in the water. His feet need to stay in the water. If he brings them up too high, he will instinctively pull his head up and swim almost vertically, which gives him a very unstable and uncertain feeling. A swim vest will usually keep your dog horizontal in the water. If he's just wearing a harness, you can put a hand under his chest for support. One small circuit with just a few doggie paddles is enough for your first time. You can still work toward your Advanced Swimmer badge tomorrow.

Swimming is very strenuous, so take lots of breaks. The younger (or older) your dog is, the longer these breaks should be!

The next day (or the one after that), walk briskly into the water. If your dog flat out refuses to come along, pick him up (if his weight allows it) and carry him into the water up to the point where he can just touch bottom,

but the water will help him float (taking the weight off your arms). Start backing up slowly so that the dog has to swim to follow you. Praise him lavishly for even a hint of a doggie paddle. Keep an arm's length between you and your dog so he doesn't accidentally scratch you with his toenails. Have your dog swim one circle around you, and then you and he can leave the water together. Bravo! If you practice swimming this way for a few sessions, your dog will soon think water is the best thing ever.

Olympic swimmers don't just fall out of the sky, but swimming as a shared activity where your dog has to rely on you is a sensational trust-building exercise.

17

BUILD A SANDBOX

Dogs love sand because they love to dig, and they *really* love to bury things and dig them up again. Having a sandbox for your dog will protect your garden and your flower beds! Even if it disturbs the look of your yard a little, it still beats having deep craters in your lawn.

If you have a smaller dog, you can even put a child's turtle sandbox on your balcony and fill it with play sand from a home improvement store. And yes, you will find sand in his coat (and in your hall, in the kitchen, in your bed ...), but your dog will be all the happier for it.

18

MENTAL COMMUNICATION
(JUST SHUT UP FOR A WHILE)

Animals can expand our understanding of life. The animals we know best are especially good teachers because they have communicative abilities that we lost long ago — probably as our spoken language kept getting better and more complex. Animals have a sixth sense. Researchers have discovered that birds who find food are quickly joined by scores of other birds summoned by a kind of "mute food call." Similar findings have been made for herd animals that spook because one animal in the vicinity senses danger; the entire herd suddenly feels a silent impulse to flee. Over and over, dog and cat owners, in particular, find that their pets know when they're coming home, even if the times are highly variable and random. My family always told me that my miniature whippet routinely went to the window 20 minutes before I got home from my errands to wait for me. Dogs and cats can find their way home even when they are hundreds of miles away. Some dogs react before their master has even put the dog whistle in his mouth and come running.

Neurologist Vladimir Bekhterev (1857–1927) was the first to study telepathic communication between man and dog and came to the conclusion that dogs can be influenced by mental suggestion. Blind people frequently report that their guide dogs know their intentions before any signals or commands are given. These invisible bonds between man and dog extend in both directions, of course, but people don't pay as much attention to the telepathic signals of their dogs — primarily because we rely on words.

Today, telepathic abilities are not nurtured but instead written off as non-sense. After all, we have the telephone now, so we don't have to concern ourselves with the power of our thoughts.

Scientific research of telepathy in animals is still in its earliest phases, but many scientists are convinced that it does constitute one aspect of social communication in groups. Animals in a group communicate with each other through body language, but primarily use pictures. Because we are constantly striving to better understand our dogs, it only makes sense to communicate mentally with your own dog. Start with baby steps: before you do something with your dog, send him a mental picture of it. For example, before you brush him, imagine the dog brush and "send" him a picture of it. See if he is less surprised than usual when you approach him with the brush in your hand. Before you clip his nails, "send" him a picture of the clippers in your hand and his paw. Do the same when you're going to take him somewhere in the car. Or remove a tick: prepare him for it using pictures in your head instead of words to tell him what you'll do. If you get the feeling that things are working well, try getting your dog to look at you during a walk solely via a mental image. If you call your dog and he hesitates, imagine him running to you with a big smile on his face – try it!

Sending mental pictures requires practice. It doesn't work right away, and it also doesn't work if you are distracted, afraid, or under a lot of stress.

However, with practice, you can learn to overcome your own mental stress or fear and still send focused images to your dog. Even if it sounds a little crazy or esoteric, just give it a try. Explain to your dog in mental images what you expect of him. If your dog is fearful and insecure, imagine him over and over as a confident, relaxed dog. If you're not at home and your errands take longer than expected, imagine your dog lying calmly and quietly on his bed (and not off-the-charts excited that you're about to come back).

And when you've perfected this technique on your dog, try it on your significant other. *That's* the real challenge.

19

ROW, ROW, ROW YOUR BOAT

Make your dog a legendary pirate – take him out in a rowboat! Even if both of you are initially uneasy on the dark water above the murky depths, this is your chance to show each other how brave, daring, and fearless you are. Your dog will be able to tell his friends tales of true adventure, of dark, stormy voyages and fierce, epic battles with the denizens of the deep.

Is the spirit of a true Captain Ahab slumbering in your dog? Try it and see!

20

FIND YOUR KEYS

Let's be honest: everyone loses his keys at some point. Some develop their talent early in life, while it comes along later in others. Why not make your dog your comfort in your old age? Your chances of finding your lost keys (gloves, hat, scarf, etc.) improve enormously when you teach your dog to look for your keys and bring them to you.

First, you have to make sure that your dog can easily find and fetch your keys. Take a cotton handkerchief that has been in your pants pocket for at least an hour (so it has your scent) and knot it around the keys or key chain your keys are on.

Play a regular game of fetch with the keys and your dog. Shake the keys excitedly and throw them a little further away. Praise your dog for showing

any interest in the keys. As soon as he picks up the keys, say "Keys!" and trade him for a treat – so he actually brings the keys to you instead of burying them somewhere else.

Once you've had several successful practice sessions and your dog has become a master key-fetcher, the next step is to start hiding the keys. Start with very easy hiding places, because this stage is about linking the search with the command "Where are the keys?" The next step is to discreetly hide the keys between various objects and tell your dog "Find the keys!" If your dog brings you something else instead, don't correct him; just repeat your command "Find the keys!" Praise him when he does it correctly.

Next, practice "accidentally" dropping your keys while you're walking. As soon as your dog picks up the keys and follows you with them, praise him to the moon! Then wait until he gets ahead of you or is doing something else, and quietly put your keys down on the edge of the sidewalk. Call him with "Find the keys!" When he finds them, congratulate him – and yourself: Now you have a true helper around the house.

21

MAKE YOUR DOG ICE CREAM

When the sun is beating down, your dog would also love to cool off. These ice cream recipes are a fabulous way to keep your dog cool, and they come together in a snap. Empty yogurt containers, silicone muffin cups, or disposable shot glasses all make great doggie ice cream containers. You can put a bully stick or rawhide stick in the middle as your "popsicle stick."

LIVERWURST-YOGURT ICE CREAM

Whisk plain low-fat or nonfat yogurt with liverwurst or braunschweiger in a 2:1 ratio and pour into ice cream cups. Insert half of a bully stick or a chicken chewy stick into each cup and place the cups in the freezer. To make it easier to get the ice cream out, briefly warm the cup in your hand.

FRUIT-YOGURT ICE CREAM

Mix plain low-fat or nonfat yogurt with pureed banana and/or apple, some kiwi and/or strawberries in a blender. Depending on how much liquid you have, add 1 to 2 teaspoons of honey. Stick a chewy stick in the middle of each cup and place them in the freezer.

You can also use cottage cheese in place of the yogurt.

LACTOSE-FREE ICE CREAM

Whisk 2 tablespoons of liverwurst with 1 cup water (or use beef or chicken stock, if you like). Add pieces of goat cheese, cooked chicken bits, or cooked liver pieces and pour the mixture into ice cream cups.

For dogs that tend to gulp down the entire cup at once without chewing, try filling a cow hoof or a Kong (a hollow rubber dog toy) and freeze – but there will be less mess if you use something with a more solid consistency, such as:

· Tuna with baby food such as pureed carrots (e.g., Gerber)
· Ground beef with veggies and parmesan cheese
· Cream cheese with pureed bananas, oats, and a little honey

22

MAKE YOUR DOG A CLOTH ROPE TOY

Small dogs are especially fond of soft cloth toys they can shake and chew on. You can make wonderful toys yourself out of old towels, fabric leftovers, or cleaning rags. Cut your material into long strips. Take three strips and knot them together at one end, and then braid the strips.

To spice it up even more, weave little treats or other goodies into your braid. When you get to the end, just make another tight knot. You should have a braided "rope" in your hand with treats hidden in it.

Let the fun begin! Put on some airs with the toy: start a game of tug-of-war and observe the surprised look on your dog's face when he notices that his new toy is really something special!

23

PRAISE YOUR DOG FOR ONCE!
(THE BEST EXERCISE OF ALL)

Most of us tend to comment on things we find bad or annoying, but remain silent about things we like. And when we deal with our dogs, we tend to talk only about the things the dog should NOT do – so the dog is getting primarily negative talk, if he is being spoken to at all. For once, do exactly the opposite! Take your dog for a walk and praise *everything* he does that you like.

He'll run ahead of you and sniff, lift his leg on something, but then maybe throw you a glance – *that's* something you like, so praise him for it. He continues on, disappears into the bushes, which you really don't like – but when he emerges again, *that's* something you like, so praise him. If you're on a walk and he decides to come to you to check in without you calling him – *that's* something you like, and a really nice move on his part, so praise him for it. If your dog runs far ahead of you, don't say anything or call him, just turn and go in the opposite direction. If he decides on his own to follow you at that point, praise him, because that shows his willingness to orient himself to you. Anything he does that demonstrates that he is paying attention to you gets praise, but not a ticker-tape parade: we don't want to create an amped-up party atmosphere, we just want to show our appreciation.

If you do this exercise for several days in a row, you'll see your dog offering more behaviors you like and fewer behaviors you normally correct him for. And you didn't ask him to do anything at all! If we repeatedly praise a behavior that a dog offers, we strengthen that behavior with our praise, and he will do it more often in the future. This exercise also creates a relaxed, peaceful atmosphere, and the walk will be much more pleasant for both of you. From now on, go for a walk and pay attention only to the positive things – and change the whole game in the bargain.

24

HAVE A PICNIC

I don't know if this is true of you, too, but as a kid, I loved going on picnics. (As an adult, not so much, because picnics for big groups are so *much work* and you have to schlep so much stuff around – and I am really too lazy to bother.)

Dogs love picnics just as much. And the best part is that you don't have to schlep silverware, dishes, or wine glasses anywhere because your dog will gladly eat directly out of your hand or off the ground.

You can have your picnic wherever you like, from a secluded clearing to a big meadow in a park (but maybe not right next to a dog-dense area, in case your dog is not good at sharing his yummies), on the beach, on a park bench – or in your own backyard.

Pack roast beef sandwiches, hot dogs, homemade dog biscuits (see below), maybe even chicken hearts – whatever your dog might go wild for. Don't forget to pack whatever you would like to eat as well. And don't forget a bottle of water and a plastic bowl – you can drink from the bottle, but your dog really shouldn't.

After you eat, play together, read, relax, and forget all your troubles for a while.

THE EASIEST DOG TREATS IN THE WORLD:

Roll out frozen puff pastry sheets and coat them with a mixture of drained canned tuna and cream cheese.

Roll up, cut into slices, and place on parchment paper on a baking sheet. Bake according to the puff pastry package directions.

By the way, this also tastes great with ingredients that people like to eat!

25

CHANGE THE MOOD

As a good dog commander – and if that sounds too warlike, then substitute dog parent, friend of dogs, leader – you are responsible for how good, how bad, and how safe your dog feels. Because he takes his lead from you, you have to set an example. You have to show him how he should feel and thus, how he should behave. What does that mean? If you are afraid, aggressive, unsure, or nervous, you can't expect your dog to react any differently (it's not for nothing that we say the apple doesn't fall far from the tree). Moods are contagious. If your partner comes home from work in a bad mood, his or her mood will quickly spread to everyone else. If a child is laughing hysterically, it's almost impossible not to laugh along. If a film is sad, and the music is too, and a dog loses his home, we immediately cry for him – unless we actively resist being infected by this mood. No one forces us to take on someone else's bad mood. There is no reason to let your mood be spoiled by someone who randomly insults you on the street.

Just as we absorb others' moods, all of our moods are passed along to our dogs. So it's totally up to you whether you and your dog are swept into whatever your current mood is – or whether you actively work to change it so that you and your dog can both enjoy a peaceful, relaxed day.
When we have a crazy, hectic day, we tend to "perpetrate" the walk the same way. We walk with more tension, walk a little faster, and we are less patient. As a result, the dog is more likely to be wound up during the walk,

he may bark at other dogs – and really let loose with joggers and cyclists and any "special" stimuli like strollers, skateboards, or people with hats.

Bring peace to your walk: go slower, dawdle a little, and make a conscious effort to breathe slowly. Sing a children's song. Dial it down. It's not about covering a certain distance to wear you and your dog out. A walk should relax you, not exasperate you. Even if going slowly drives you nuts at first because you are used to covering the world in gigantic strides: who knows? Perhaps you will suddenly develop a deeply relaxed eye for the little things in life – the birds, the moths, the mouse tracks in the snow.

If you are nice and relaxed, but your dog is shooting around like a rocket for some reason, put him on a ten-foot line and deliberately walk slowly. And if you should encounter, say, a cat or your dog's arch-enemy, the dog from across the street, stand still, turn your shoulders away from the enemy of the moment, and thus away from the stimulus, and do – *nothing*. Think about something incredibly boring such as a yawner of a wedding toast, a politician's long-winded speech, or a truly terrible hot dog commercial. It works, you'll see! When your dog doesn't get any attention for his excitement, the whole thing suddenly becomes a lot less important (you may be familiar with this strategy from your mother-in-law). Don't walk on until your dog has "come down" again. That will allow him to take this last peaceful impression of this place along with him. In dogs, the last impression counts more than the first, which means that the next time you are at this spot, he won't immediately revert to his previous keyed-up state and look for the cat or the stupid nemesis dog.

26

THE RIGHT BALANCE

The secret to a happy life, for both dogs and humans, is balance. Not too much of anything, but enough of everything: enough food, enough quiet, enough work, play, love and affection. Dogs love those quiet moments of relaxation with us just as much as the praise we heap on them for what they do. To a dog, a morning outside in the sun with his owner by his side is just as important and meaningful as an adventure that he works his way through. It's all about timing.

Find out what the right balance for *your* dog is … and maybe that's the right balance for you, too. Because that's certainly one of the things we can learn from our dogs: when it's the right time to run around, and when the moment has come to rest.

27

TAKE A SIESTA TOGETHER

Sharing your bed with your dog has its drawbacks: even if you ignore the sand and pine needles and the significant drop in available space, even the tiniest dogs suddenly become enormous dinosaurs in bed, hogging the pillow and most of the blanket for themselves. On the other hand, the benefits of sharing your bed with your dog are scientifically proven (you'd almost think that dogs commissioned this study): First, dogs are living hot water bottles whose body temperatures stay at a toasty 100 degrees Fahrenheit. This is a not insignificant reason why noble ladies 200 years ago brought their dogs into bed – it was simply impossible to sufficiently heat their castles. But, warmth aside, when you and your dogs cuddle in your sleep, you all give off oxytocin, the "love hormone" that deepens your bond with each other. Just three minutes of cuddling increases blood oxytocin levels in both humans and dogs – which makes it much easier for you to get along. A British study from 2010 also shows that petting a dog is one of the best ways to relieve stress – far better than a glass of wine. Not to mention that petting a dog doesn't give you heartburn or a headache! According to this study, people who spend time with a dog after a long, hard day are more relaxed, more optimistic, and less burdened by everyday problems.

And besides: unlike human snoring, the *soft* snoring of your beloved dog is relaxing and helps you sleep, too.

28

BRING ME A TISSUE!

Many dogs LOVE to fetch things. If you are lucky enough to have such a dog, use his talents to your advantage! This exercise is not only a sensational party trick, it is invaluable if you have the flu.

Start by putting a cloth handkerchief or a paper towel on the floor and use the command "Bring it!" (or whatever your normal fetch command is) to get him to bring it to you. For the first few sessions, it helps if you're not very far away from the item and you point directly at it. If he won't pick it up, try holding it right in front of him at nose level. If he takes it then, say "Hurray!" and give him a cookie. The next step is to lay it at your feet, and then gradually move it further away from you. Once your dog understands that he should bring you the small white thing, add the command "Bring me a tissue!"

Once that works, advance to the next step: put an open package of tissues on the floor or a low side table so he can pull a tissue from the box.

The only disadvantage to teaching your dog this trick is that you have to put all the tissues up out of reach when you don't need them. If you forget, you may find tissues all over your house in various stages of destruction...

29

TO CONQUER THE HEART OF YOUR DEAREST DOG ONCE AND FOR ALL: MAYDAY LIVER TOFFEES

If nothing else is working, your adolescent dog is stuck in Mayday! Mayday! mode and you no longer know up from down, if your dog seems listless, if you need a reward, but don't want to ruin your diet and are therefore willing to do a good deed for your dog – THAT'S when you need liver toffees made from nutritious liver and bacon.

Ingredients for liver toffees
(makes approximately 95 pieces):
· 1 pound chicken or lamb liver
· 1½ cups cold water
· 3 cups all-purpose flour (for dogs who cannot tolerate wheat, replace the flour with buckwheat flour or chickpea flour)
· 4 strips turkey bacon, cooked and cut into small pieces
· 1 egg
· ⅓ cup olive oil

Preparation:
Preheat oven to 350°F. Line a 9x13 casserole dish with parchment paper. Combine the liver and water in a food processor and puree. Add to a large bowl with the flour, bacon, egg and olive oil until it forms a stiff dough. Distribute the dough in the casserole dish and bake on the middle rack of the oven for 30 to 35 minutes. When a toothpick or knife inserted into the center comes out clean, the toffee is cooked. Place the pan on a rack and allow to cool.

Using a sharp knife, cut the toffee into small cubes about ¾ across. Divide the toffees up into numerous small bags and place in the freezer – this will let you thaw and feed fresh pieces on a regular basis. Due to their residual moisture, the toffees will not keep long outside the freezer and should be fed to your dog within 24 hours of being thawed.

30

NERVE FOOD FOR DOGS

Even dogs can get a little testy if they haven't eaten for a while or if they have too few carbohydrates in their diet (in dogs, we call it "poor impulse control," but men who haven't had breakfast are just "hangry").
Fearful and/or nervous dogs in particular profit greatly from high-quality carbohydrates at breakfast, as preparation before a training session, or as a snack on high-stress days.

Oats are one of the healthiest grains and the only one that contains all nine amino acids. It is also an excellent source of important nutrients and vitamins; it contains a lot of biotin, vitamin B1 (the nerve vitamin!) as well as B6, iron, magnesium, silicon, and antioxidants.

GOOD MOOD BREAD
Ingredients:
· 8 cups organic rolled oats
· 3 cups plain low-fat Greek yogurt
· ⅓ cup ground flaxseed
· 12 oz grass-fed ground beef or one 12-oz can of chunk light tuna in water or 12 oz salmon
· 2 tbsp organic coconut oil
· 1 handful of fresh herbs (parsley, basil, dandelion greens, tarragon, etc.)
· as much water as needed (the dough should be easy to knead)

Preparation:
Mix all ingredients and knead the dough into a ball. Depending on the size of the dog, separate into individual round pieces that are golf-ball size to tennis ball-size.

Let the treats dry for about two hours in a 300°F oven, until they are nice and hard. Turn off the oven, open the oven door, and let them cool in the oven.

Keep your treats in cloth bags – due to their residual moisture, they will get moldy in plastic containers or bags. In cloth or fabric bags, they will keep for about a month – assuming your dog doesn't eat them all immediately!

31

TRY CLICKER TRAINING

Clicker training is a very effective training method that enables a person to "mark" a dog's desirable behavior at the precise moment it occurs. It is also used on chickens, horses, bulls, and even fish! The clicker itself is a plastic cricket-type noisemaker that makes a distinct "click" sound when you press it. The trick is to click at the exact moment when your dog obeys a command or just does something right. Because this sound is new and unusual, the dog can immediately link the sound to his behavior, especially if a reward follows the click. The click becomes a promise of a cookie to follow, and the dog knows exactly what he did to earn the click, which means he will repeat the desired behavior.

When you are teaching a new behavior, you need to have your clicker with you at every training session, but your dog usually progresses much more quickly than with other methods because the click makes the message much clearer for the dog. (This is why top gymnasts also use clickers, by the way: the coach can mark precisely when the gymnast's body is completely straight. If he has to say it out loud, the moment has already passed.)

Proper timing is absolutely essential when you use a clicker. You must click at the precise moment when the dog is displaying the desired behavior and then immediately reward the dog.

Once your dog has learned a behavior to the point of mastery, you can slowly fade the treat after the click for that particular behavior.

By the way, clickers also motivate you, the human trainer, to concentrate on desirable behavior instead of focusing on mistakes to be corrected. This makes it much more fun and much less frustrating to teach your dog something new.

32

DISCOVERY TRAIL

If you have a dog who doesn't (yet) know how to play, or one who is old and doesn't want to play anymore, or a young dog who is bored, or a dog who already knows all the toys you have in the house – build him a discovery trail. You can use a hall, your driveway, your backyard, your balcony, or any surface with some space where you won't mind if it gets wet.

Much like you did in the "Dive deep" chapter, prepare three bowls with differently flavored water (one bowl could have water with a slice of roast beef in it, the second could have an anchovy at the bottom, and the third could have some sunflower oil in it, for example) and place them on your trail. A few feet further on, put down a big plastic bag and hide two or three treats underneath it. At another spot, crumple up a big bath towel and hide small pieces of smoked herring in a few of the folds. Somewhere along the way, add a large or small stuffed animal that crackles, one that your dog has never seen before (most department stores have terrific moose, deer, or panda toys – or wonderful crackling baby toys). A little further on, put out an empty toilet paper roll and put half a peeled hard-boiled egg inside the roll. Next, put out an old rubber boot or colander and hide a piece of cheese underneath it. (It doesn't matter if your dog likes eggs and cheese or not: it's about the different scents.) Build a multi-station discovery course that will excite all of your dog's senses: he should sniff, look, listen, and taste. The big stuffed animal might fall over, and the toilet paper makes a funny sound when you want to get something out of it. There are hard and soft objects that your dog can move or rummage through with his paw or nose to get the cookies, and sometimes he might have to gather his courage *and* be inventive to get at the individual treats.

You are a spectator, nothing more. Your dog can discover and explore this olfactory slice of heaven all by himself. You don't need to put anything away until he shows no further interest in any of the objects. Depending on the size of the course you've built, that could take half an hour!

33

JUMP ON A TRAMPOLINE

Today, many people with children and a backyard have large platform trampolines with a thick net all around the outside so that no one can be bounced off the edge like a ball. If you know someone who has a trampoline like this, ask if you can get on it with your dog! Don't start by jumping up and down. Just watch your dog walk unsteadily on the curiously yielding surface. Once he seems a little more sure of himself, you can start taking tiny hops to make the trampoline bounce a little. Tell your dog something funny while you do this (your talking is actually calming for him here) to motivate him to join in. The more sure-footed your dog becomes on the trampoline, the higher you can bounce. Terriers in particular tend to enthusiastically play along. If your dog keeps getting braver and wilder, you can add a Kong or Jolly Egg to the mix, which guarantees even more fun: just try catching an egg-shaped ball on a trampoline!

34

TAKE A BEACH VACATION

Somewhere near you, there must be a beach of some kind – along a river, at a lake, on the sea.

Dogs love the beach. There's just something about it – the sand? Open space? Wind? Water? – that makes dogs go totally insane. They get the zoomies, they play in the sand, they bury themselves in it, they charge into the water and back out again and then run in circles around you while simultaneously shaking themselves. And then they get another attack of the zoomies, and repeat, until eventually, drunk on fresh air and exultation, they plop down on the sand, panting and grinning, with sand on their faces, noses, coats, and between their toes.

For extra bonus points, go on a beach vacation for a few days – you and your dog. During peak season, it's hard to get accommodations on a good beach with your dog: dog beaches are usually right next to the nude beaches (no one was able to tell me why), and that's a situation you have to be able to handle. But there are also vacation homes with private beaches that welcome canine guests. Otherwise, plan your trip in the spring or fall instead. Dogs like it just as much – or more, because the sand isn't so hot. And humans can experience an amazing atmosphere at the beach that might inspire you to write poems or finish your first novel. Who knows?

35

A MIXTAPE FOR YOUR DOG

Decades ago, we used to make mixtapes for people we really cared about. For those of you who only know cassettes from old movies or the technology museum: making a mixtape entailed hours of painstaking work recording songs onto a cassette. And if there was a message recorded with titles like "Light my fire," "I wanna be loved by you" or "You take me higher," it was pretty clear what the giver wanted to tell you.

Happily, dogs don't care about song lyrics, so you don't have to worry about trying to send a message: to them, it's all about the music itself. But your choices do matter. You're not normally going to thrill a dog with Whitesnake, Rammstein or Metallica. They like to hear upbeat music, songs with a strong melody line, or mathematically structured music like Bach.

Music also has therapeutic effects: newly acquired dogs, very nervous dogs or dogs that have a hard time calming down, dogs with separation anxiety, puppies, and dog owners all have been proven to benefit greatly from classical music. However, just turning on the radio usually doesn't help much, because people tend to talk excitedly between the songs, or there are ads with doorbells ringing, dogs barking, cats meowing, children's voices, etc.

Instead of the radio, make a mixtape 2.0 for your dog. The following pieces have been tested on both my own dogs and "guest" dogs in our absence and proven to be calming. Assemble this playlist on an iPod and play it in an endless loop when you leave the house, a dog needs to heal after an operation, there's a thunderstorm, or any similar situation.

Vivaldi: "Winter" (Largo)
Beethoven: "Pathétique," Sonata Op. 13: Adagio Cantabile
Schumann: "Träumerei"
Bach: "Sarabande" in D Minor
Brahms: "Intermezzo" in D Major
J.S. Bach: "Arioso"
Beethoven: Moonlight Sonata
Brahms: Intermezzo in D Major, Opus 116 No. 4
Chopin: Valse mélancolique in F Sharp Minor
Schubert: Sonata in A Major, A D959, Adagio
Debussy: "Sarabande"
Rachmaninof: "Vocalise" Op. 34 No. 14
Händel: "Sarabande" in D Minor
Karganoff: "Arabesque"
Beethoven: "Gertrude's Dream Waltz"

36

TRAIN AN EMERGENCY WHISTLE SIGNAL

An emergency whistle or emergency command can be a lifesaver for your dog, even if he is usually on a leash. When your dog is going somewhere he absolutely should not go, or if you need to rescue him from a dangerous situation, or when he's chasing after something or charging up to something, this command means he should immediately turn around and run back to you at the same rate of speed. That's why I also call it the "turn-around" whistle.

The turn-around whistle has to be trained differently from a "normal" command because it must also be able to call the dog off instinctual behaviors like charging or harassing other animals.

If you're not good at making a piercing whistle with your fingers, buy and use a dog whistle for this command. Just make sure you always have it on you so you can react to the unexpected. You can also use a loud yodel-like call or a high-pitched "Brrrr" sound – in the end, it's up to you (or your dog) which sound will provoke the best response. Try different ideas: some dogs react wonderfully to a dog whistle, while others respond to a totally crazy sound. The important thing is that everyone who will walk the dog can make the same noise or sound.

WHAT WILL YOUR DOG DO ANYTHING FOR?

On a day when your dog is still a bit hungry (maybe in the afternoon before the evening meal, if he eats two meals a day, or after only half of his breakfast), you need to pack something that your dog would truly do anything for. It has to be something truly spectacular, way more than just a reward: like Christmas, his birthday, and Thanksgiving put together. It has to be soft, juicy, fatty if possible, and something you can break into many tiny pieces – so preferably nothing dry. Consider cheese, liverwurst, bologna, cold cut bits, little liverwurst sandwiches – many dogs would gladly die for watermelon, while others would sell their souls for pizza, and most dogs would run until their legs gave out for roast chicken. Whatever it is, it has to be a jackpot.

At the very beginning of your walk, stand in front of your dog and whistle softly – he's right in front of you, so you don't need to be loud – and let a handful of your jackpot item fall to the ground. Now he knows that the whistle means good stuff will follow.

Continue your walk, and when the dog gets out in front of you – when he's just trotting along, calm, and relaxed – then, with no warning at all, whistle, turn around, and run in the opposite direction with a big grin on your face until your dog catches you. Then stand still, praise him to the skies, and have an exuberant party: rain delicious rewards down from the heavens and celebrate like crazy! You're letting the jackpot "rain" down from above because scent-oriented dogs in particular love to sniff out and find each tasty treat on their own.

Repeat this procedure again during your walk: whistle, run away, party, but remember, whistle only when your dog is in motion, never when he is still.

You can practice this exercise twice a day, but only two or three days of the week. Do your first ten practice whistles just as I described above. It is important when you do this that there are no distractions nearby so you can be sure your dog will be successful. It's always a good idea to look around carefully before you whistle and turn around to sprint away – otherwise you might knock over a jogger and pelt him with bologna.

After your first ten practice whistles, do the next ten without any distraction as well – but now, instead of running in the opposite direction, you will just walk quickly in the other direction. As soon as the dog, who knows how the game works at this point, gets to you, throw another huge and enthusiastic party. However, from whistle to whistle, you will slowly reduce the amount of roast chicken and insane cheering – but it should still be a noteworthy event.

Once you've made it to whistle number 20, whistle, walk three or four steps in the other direction until the dog reaches you – then give him three pieces of your jackpot item, a "What a gooooood boy!" – and that's it. If that sounds disappointing after all those parties, well, that's life. People congratulate you when you first get your driver's license, but once you know how to drive, you won't see a policeman running up to you at an intersection with a huge bouquet of flowers just because you're a good driver. So as you progress in your training, you have to cut back on the birthday-party-level food and excitement, because neither you nor your dog should become dependent on the jackpot.

But when you use your whistle or command for the first time in a true emergency situation and your dog breaks away from chasing a deer (or a mountain biker, if that's the equivalent for your particular dog), you can throw a gigantic party and squeal wildly and give him two whole roast chickens, if you want.

If your dog is too unreliable to be off-leash, you can practice your turn-around whistle on a long line. Let the long line fall to the ground and run away at the same time you whistle to avoid getting your hands jerked if your dog doesn't react right away. Once your dog has returned to you and is happily gobbling down his jackpot, just put the long line back into your hand.

If you build the command in this way, your dog eventually won't even consider any other option besides running to you when he hears the whistle.

Once your dog has sufficient practice with the command, introduce a mild distraction, then a moderate one, and then a really tough one (a mild distraction is often one that is very far away). If you keep to this sequence, you can successfully call nine out of ten dogs off a wild animal this way.

For the next twelve years, you should make it a habit to practice the whistle once or twice a month as a fun game: it's not a program that is forever burned onto the dog's hard drive – and it is really not a simple thing to short-circuit a dog's instinctive behavior. So you have to keep practicing unusual behaviors and "stay fit" so that the whistle will work when you need it.

37

GET IN THE POOL

Most dogs love water once the weather heats up. Even dogs who normally shun vigorous swimming can certainly get something out of a leisurely paddle when the temps get high enough. So if you have a backyard or a balcony, you can do your dog a big favor and set up an inflatable kiddie pool for him. Many dogs will wallow in it throughout the dog days of summer and cool off their bellies, feet, and rear end.

You can get kiddie pools at a home improvement store, department stores, and most larger drugstores. If you have a dog with large toenails, try to get one with an inflatable bottom – not so you can blow it up, but because it is double-walled and therefore stronger.

38

PLAY HIDE-AND-SEEK

Because most dogs love looking for things, they also love playing hide-and-seek. There are lots of possibilities here. Start by hiding treats in a room of your house for your dog (but don't let him see you hide them unless he's a puppy): under the sofa, on a bookshelf, under a towel, on an armchair, in a bowl, behind the TV – whatever is appropriate for your dog's size and physical ability. For a Labrador Retriever, who doesn't really care if things get broken, you should be extra careful if you hide treats behind wobbly objects.

If this game works well, you can play hide-and-seek with some of your dog's favorite toys. Such toys generally have a special strong scent of their own and are therefore easily sniffed out and found. With your dog blocked from entering the room, hide the toy on the lowest shelf of a bookshelf on

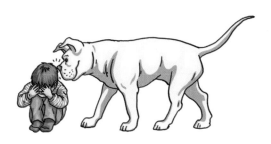

top of the books – but in such a way that he doesn't immediately see it when he comes back in. Or put it on the seat of a chair that's pushed under the table. Or under an armchair so that one part of the toy is still peeking out and the dog can grab it once he finds it.

The better your dog gets, the harder the hiding places you can use. Instead of putting it *on* the books on the bookshelf, put it *behind* the books on the shelf, etc.

There is also a variation involving kids. You just need a few kids your dog knows and plenty of space. Hide the kids in a cabinet, behind armchairs or sofas, under tables, lying still on a table, on the kitchen counter, or in a closet. Tell your dog the name of the child he should find. If he's confused, have the child make an odd noise, repeating if necessary. When he finds the child, a giant giggle attack, cackling while rolling around on the floor, and licking the child's face are all definitely allowed!

39

HAPPY BIRTHDAY

Even when it's abundantly clear that dogs really don't care much about their birthdays, there's really no such thing as celebrating too much, don't you agree?

This recipe – no matter when or for what occasion you want to serve it to your dog – is easy to slice and serve, just in case you want to invite a few doggie friends over for tea.

BIRTHDAY CAKE
Ingredients:
- $3/4$ lb ground lamb
- 1 $1/2$ cups all-purpose flour
- $1/2$ cup rolled oats
- $1/3$ cup ground sunflower seeds
- $1/2$ cup cottage cheese
- 2 large eggs, beaten
- $2/3$ cup of water

For the icing:
- $2/3$ cup softened cream cheese
- 1 cup cheddar cheese, shredded or cut into small pieces
- 1 tsp chopped parsley

Preparation:

Preheat the oven to 350°F.

Grease a springform pan.

In a large bowl, combine the lamb, flour, oats, the ground sunflower seeds, eggs, and ²/₃ cup water in a large bowl until it forms a dough.

Pour the dough into the springform pan and bake for approximately 45 minutes. Let the cake cool before removing it from the springform pan. "Frost" the cake with cream cheese. Decorate with the cheese and sprinkle with the chopped parsley.

Yum!

40

HE RELAXES ON COMMAND!

With any dog, you will eventually encounter a situation where he is under terrible stress and hardly knows up from down. Even the calmest, quietest, most perfectly socialized dogs can become terrified in unforeseen situations. A dog owner who has developed a relaxation signal for times like this is lucky indeed. The signal immediately tells the dog how he can behave in a better, i.e., more relaxed manner.

Conditioning a relaxation signal is incredibly easy: whenever your dog happens to be super relaxed – because you're rubbing his tummy, massaging him with closed eyes, or when he's wonderfully tired after a long walk – speak softly to him and murmur the same word over and over again. Many people use the word "easy" because you can draw out the vowels and make the word wonderfully long: "eeeeeeeeeeeasyyyyyyyyyyyy." Others like "quiiiiiiiiiiiiiet." But you can say "yuppyguppypuppy" or whatever else you want. The important thing is that you always say the same thing whenever your dog is deeply relaxed. You can also link the word to a specific scent (like lavender or a relaxing mix of essential oils) and/or a specific blanket or bed so you can better convey the relaxation/safety signal at a place like the vet's. When your dog repeatedly hears the same word, smells the same special scent, and feels the same blanket or bed, he will automatically link a feeling of comfort to them. In this way, you can employ one or more of these signals to quickly calm him.

So if you and your dog somehow end up in a spooky subway tunnel, or some indefinable yet unexpected object ends up at your front door, just say "easy" or "quiet" in the same tone you've used in your dry runs. You'll be amazed!

41

TEACH A SHY DOG HOW TO PLAY

Play is important. It strengthens the bond and the relationship between two beings – which is why even older dogs who are well past their zoomie days will sometimes spontaneously play with a dog or person they like. But some dogs have no idea of how to play. This is often true of dogs adopted from shelters as adults who have no experience with toys and have never learned that sometimes you are allowed to just be silly with people. Dogs who have grown up primarily with other dogs for company and who've had little contact with people generally have no idea how to play with humans. With dogs like these, you must first establish trust before you can get all silly with them: dogs have to be able to assess who you actually are before you are allowed to do something "out of character." Give yourself and your dog the time necessary to build a relationship.

Movement and speed are a good way to introduce your dog to "playing" and build interest in a toy (prey!). Moving a toy around on the floor in small zigzags or circles is also a good starting point. A cat toy on a line or a kitty rod with feathers or ribbons tied to it are fabulous yet unobtrusive ways to get an unsure dog to react to a moving object.

Don't force him to play. If he engages, keep the session short to avoid overtaxing him. Once you've got a feel for his personality and what he likes best, you can begin to build a true bond by playing in new ways together.

42

WRITE YOUR DOG A LETTER

Frederick the Great did it too. He even made his brother godfather to the puppies of his favorite greyhound bitch Biche – only to revoke the title in a fit of anger.

So, really, write your dog a letter. Write what you think of him, what happened to you the first time you saw him, when you knew that he was "your" dog. Write your favorite things about him and the things that drive you nuts. When he made you cry for the first time and why, and when he makes you laugh. Write how his fur feels and where you especially like to pet him. And write everything you always wanted to tell him.

Write it all down and keep the letter in a safe place. And the next time your dog makes you so angry that you ask yourself why you didn't invest in an aquarium instead, get the letter out and read it.

43

MAKE YOURSELF AND YOUR DOG USEFUL

Even the smallest friendly gesture makes a difference. Working together, there are many things you and your dog can do to make a difference in the lives of others, and they don't require a huge time commitment. Here are just a few possibilities:

VISIT A NURSING HOME
Dogs offer a distraction from everyday cares, are friends to those who are lonely, and bring joy, play, and fun into the day-to-day nursing home routine. A so-called "visiting dog" is not a therapy dog, because the person, not the dog, does the job. The dog just acts as a bridge. The handler doesn't have to have any particular degrees, but in Germany, handlers must complete roughly five days of training. Your local animal welfare organization can provide more information.

BLOOD DONATION
Donate your dog's blood to save other dogs' lives.
In principle, any healthy dog can donate blood as long as he fulfills the following criteria:
· free of acute or chronic diseases
· body weight of at least 30 kg/66 lb
· proof that dog is up-to-date on vaccinations
· preferably negative for DEA 1.1 and DEA 7
· calm, even temperament

Any veterinarian can draw blood. In Germany, you can find more information here: *www.weissepfoten.de*

UK: *www.petbloodbankuk.org*

USA: Talk to your veterinarian to see if your dog can donate blood, either at the vet's office or a blood bank.

CHARITY WALK
Take a walk for a good cause. Sign up for a charity dog walk and make sure you and your dog help raise awareness for that issue or cause.

ANIMAL SHELTER SPONSORSHIP
Sponsor a dog at your local animal shelter, or become a volunteer and walk shelter dogs.

SEARCH AND RESCUE (SAR) TRAINING
Train your dog to be a crisis assistance dog. After two years of training, you and your dog can help out in emergency situations.

44

SHOW YOUR DOG THAT KIDS ARE TERRIFIC PLAYMATES

Not all dogs get along well with kids right "out of the box." Some have had negative past experiences with them. However, as long as there is not irrecoverable trauma (i.e., being tortured by children for years) involved, you can help your dog become great buddies with kids. Here's how:

Find a child three or older who is used to dogs and not afraid of them. Give the child some dog treats and play "Hansel and Gretel." The child can leave a trail of cookies (or hot dog slices) – and then see if the dog can find and follow the trail!

Like most dogs, kids love bubbles. Both kids and dogs also love popping bubbles. So you just need some strong lungs to keep them amused!

Play hide-and-seek. Have your dog sit while the child goes and hides. When the dog finds the child, he gets a treat.

45

WAG MORE, BARK LESS – DOGS AS PHILOSOPHERS

Dogs teach us to greet each day with a big smile and a cheer and to love with total devotion, holding nothing back.

They forgive easily.

And they are perfectly aware of when they should run and when they should rest.

They show us that every day is a gift, and every meal is the very, very best meal ever in the history of the universe.

Let your dog's view of the world become your own. Consider him your personal four-legged philosopher. After all, we each get the dog we deserve.

46

TURN YOUR LIVING ROOM INTO A DOGGIE GYM

Especially during periods of bad weather in spring or fall (or if you live in Hamburg: in the spring, summer, fall, and of course in the winter), you're not always eager to go out in the great outdoors and exercise. On the other hand, young dogs or any terrier will get pretty bored with that.

To combat this boredom, build your dog an agility course using everyday objects you already have in your home. Be creative! I do have to warn you, though, that you have to participate a bit, so get off that couch!

Build a tunnel using a blanket thrown over some chairs. Two piles of books with a broomstick placed across them create a knee-high jump for your dog. Putting two or three long window boxes (the kind you plant flowers in) with the long sides touching creates a small broad jump. Put a hula hoop in a doorway so your dog can either jump through it or crawl

underneath it. Set up a wooden toy car that your dog has to push with his nose, and set up a line of flowerpots for your dog to weave in and out of. To show him how to do it, go with him step by step through the weaves – and give him a treat after each flowerpot! Have him "Down!" on a bathmat; at another spot, he can jump onto the seat of a chair and sit there. You can continue in this vein for as long as you like – the possibilities are endless! And should you decide to buy finished "obstacles," the Ikea children's section has play tunnels; check Craigslist or the classifieds for a ball pit and tent.

47

MAKING TRADES

Teach your dog to trade things in his mouth for something in your hand. This is an important thing to do because in a crisis, it could save your dog's life, a beloved child's toy, or the neighbor's cat.

Puppies will put anything in their mouths that isn't tied down (and sometimes even things that are), so you can get in a lot of "trade" practice. If you have small children and a puppy in your home, the puppy will probably be overwhelmed by your kids' stuffed animal collection – and you'll get to practice trading 40 times a day. As soon as he has something in his mouth you don't want in there, offer him a high-value treat, a piece of bologna or liverwurst, freeze-dried chicken, etc. Never, never, never freak out or make a scene when your dog has something in his mouth that angers or upsets you: the more excited you get, the more the dog will think that the thing he found is clearly something fantastic, something that he should keep or even swallow immediately (even though he may not have planned to do that before). Try to always keep a treat or a piece of freeze-dried meat in your pants pockets or jacket pockets so that you'll have something handy to trade if the neighbor's rabbit suddenly throws himself into your dog's mouth or he finds something strange in the bushes at the park. The fact that you have absolutely zero desire to possess what he surrenders to you is your problem, unfortunately.

48

DIG FOR TREASURE TOGETHER

Because most dogs love digging more than almost anything else, as we mentioned previously, organizing a hunt for buried treasure is sure to be a hit. This is basically the advanced version of digging a hole together.

If you have a sandbox or are vacationing at the beach, bury a few interesting things in the sand – your dog's favorite ball, a squeaky toy, a rope toy, a tennis shoe that smells like your feet, or whatever else he would be delighted to find – and invite him to dig it up.

If you search along with him, he will be surprised and enthusiastic – and he'll get even more excited when the two of you pull these interesting things out of the sand.

49

TAKING A HIKE

Going hiking is a truly wonderful thing: time recedes into the distance, and it's just you hiking with only your dog and your thoughts for company through forests, fields, meadows, or dunes, on twisty paths and broad trails, past sleepy villages and through evergreen forests.

The nicest moments in life are those that are shared: there are glorious routes you can hike with your dog. No matter where you go – a farm vacation, a tour of the Baltic, a seaside vacation, or "top dog" accommodations at a hotel – the trip is always about playing, running, and relaxing. Whether you're in an RV or just in your car – get away and leave all your cares behind!

There are plenty of guides about hiking with dogs available online or at your local bookstore, and the big dog magazines regularly run stories about traveling with your dog. The Internet also has travel agencies specifically

for people traveling with their canines. So it shouldn't be difficult to find just the right route in just the right place that is a perfect fit for both your dog and your preferences.

However, if you want to tent camp with your dog, you should probably try a dry run in your backyard or on property belonging to a friend. You will quickly find out whether your dog is capable of relaxing inside the thin tent walls at all. If he can't, you can forget about shared rest and relaxation.

50

LET YOUR "ONLY DOG" GO FOR A WALK WITH A DOG WALKER

If you have an only dog, whom you no doubt love very, very much because he is the apple of your eye, you can do him a favor by sending him on a walk with a good dog walker once a week. It's good for dogs to occasionally integrate into a group and enjoy lots of canine social contact. And it's good for your dog to walk with someone who isn't blinded by love for him but is more of a just neutral guide. That person does dog walks very differently than you do, and the group dynamics make the walk a very different experience from your familiar turns around the block. Of course, it's important to make sure that the dog walker you choose isn't someone who hates his or her job and merely marches hordes of leashed dogs through the city or to a safe off-leash area before leaving them to their own devices so he/she can chat with other dog walkers. Choose someone with many years of experience walking dogs who does interesting walks in the country or in special parks, someone who truly gets involved with the dogs. There are great dog walkers who won't take more than seven, eight, or nine dogs and make sure that the dogs all get along with each other. They truly understand dogs and dog language and don't attach everyone to a long lead like an anchor. And they don't throw dog training discs or, God forbid, chains around when a dog doesn't obey. You have to look hard to find these ideal dog walkers, but your dog is worth it. And so are you: you'll be able to nurse a cold or go to work with a clear conscience.

51

LISTEN TO YOUR GUT

If someone gives you advice about your dog that seems off or not right somehow, don't follow it. You don't have to (and should not) use a training method you don't like – even if it comes from some ultra-famous TV trainer or big-name local trainer. And if that method includes things like kicking your dog, leash pops, throwing the dog on the ground, or other stress-inducing elements, you should *absolutely* follow your gut! If your veterinarian recommends a medical procedure that seems strange to you, get a second opinion. Even vets can be wrong (or just not know enough about a certain topic). And that's true of any expert: dog trainers make mistakes or are just plain bad trainers, and sometimes "dog experts" don't know enough or know nothing at all. You know your dog best, so you are in the best position to know what is good and right for him.

52

FOR SHORT-HAIRED DOGS:
WIPE THEM WITH A DRY WASHCLOTH

Take a terry cloth washcloth that has air-dried so it's nice and stiff and rub your short-haired dog down with it for a terrific massage. This will work even on shy or fearful dogs who aren't quite sure what they think about intense bodily contact. Just rub away – it seems to be at least as comfortable as rolling around on the carpet.

53

FOR LONGER-HAIRED DOGS: HAIR SLIDES

If your dog has longer hair, pull gently on individual hairs or thin bunches of strands without yanking or pinching. In a very short amount of time, your dog will relax completely and close his eyes in bliss. While you work, firmly resist any temptation to remove any burrs, tangles, or anything else from your dog's fur. This is not the time for that. Hair slides are solely about wellness and relaxation.

54

BECOME A POSITIVE THINKER

Now that you know that your mood has a direct impact on your dog, you can take advantage of your walks to more or less instantly become a better, more interested, more open human being. Instead of just walking along, observe other human-dog pairs. For every pair that you see, think about why the owner might have picked out this specific dog. Was it the incredibly hilarious ears that the approaching German Shepherd mix wears like a bishop's miter that made him so irresistible to his new owner? Was it that dog's expression of total confidence and absolute authority that made the gentleman over there decide on his terrier? Was it the floating gait of the Afghan Hound that so enchanted his mistress that she decided against her better judgment to accept the lifelong time-consuming coat care duties that came with it? Was it the wise, knowing look in his eyes that made your neighbor adopt her senior dog from the shelter? Does the petite woman feel safer with that giant herding/protection dog at the end of her leash? How did that huge, muscle-bound guy find room in his heart for seven teeny tiny teacup dogs?

You'll see that you approach strange dogs and their people in a much more friendly and positive manner when you think about what may have moved them to share their lives with a specific dog. And then, when some owner lets his giant, clumsy young dog run full tilt up to your small and somewhat unsure dog, maybe you'll be in the mood to assume that he just wasn't expecting it – or was just distracted, or has a headache. Usually, such incidents are not malicious at all; the other party just can't see the possible consequences. So just put yourself between the approaching dog and your own without getting angry; this will significantly relax the situation for everyone involved. And walking your dog should never ruin your mood or your day.

55

MAKE A CONSCIOUS EFFORT TO WALK SLOWLY

You know that you are the one who sets the pace for your walks with your dog. If you are hectic, it will be a hectic walk. If you are restless, your dog will become nervous too. Sometimes we make our dogs nervous or jumpy because we constantly move like we are fleeing the scene of a crime and march along with giant steps.

If you catch yourself starting to steer your walk in this unhealthy direction because you or your dog lack inner peace, deliberately slow your pace. Dawdle. Stroll along very slowly like you're looking for some keys you lost. Calm your breathing. Stand still and just look around you – even if it's just an intersection or a riverbank. It's okay: a bit of rubbernecking never hurt anyone, on the contrary. And taking a stand during your walk also has something nice about it as long as it doesn't become a habit. It certainly removes the rushed feel from your walk. And that just makes it that much nicer and more relaxing when you do start moving along again.

56

TAKE A PAGE OUT OF YOUR DOG'S BOOK:
LET THE PAST GO

We dog lovers never get tired of talking about how great it is that dogs always live in the "here and now" and don't give a whit about yesterday or tomorrow. Sadly, however, we don't seem to adopt this excellent quality ourselves. After all, living in the here and now means that you don't let old hurts determine the course of your life. It doesn't matter what kind of history you're carrying around. If you look carefully, almost everyone has a bad childhood or bad things that happened to them, everyone has parents they didn't deserve, and if it's not parents, then it's a teacher or some other relative or just bad circumstances that are at fault for everything.

Dogs are completely free of such feelings – otherwise it would not be possible to take abused, starving, and unsocialized creatures and turn them back into strong, free, and trustworthy dogs who not only manage day-to-day life quite nicely, but take on new tasks and even high-responsibility jobs like therapy dog, drug search dog, and family pet (the hardest job of all!). And dogs don't spend their lives crippling themselves with self-pity because pity is a terrible way to express love. Pity doesn't help the recipient move forward; it gives him the feeling that he's "different from the others," and something's wrong with him. Pity blocks your view of the other person's actual personality. You only see their supposed misery – but the whole person is so much more. A dog, too, is much, much more than his sad story, his amputated leg, his missing eye. Pity often prevents us from recognizing our dog's true personality. We don't guide him the way we should; for example, we don't set proper limits for him because we feel so sorry for him after everything he has been through. But when we don't set limits for him, he's in a kind of free fall because he doesn't know what is allowed and what is not. It's a lot like a blind person left alone in a huge open space: he won't feel secure until he reaches the walls, the edges of the room, and he can feel his way along them.

Forget your dog's sad past. Focus on giving him a happy, secure present instead.

57

COOKING FOR EVERYONE! CHICKEN AND PEARL BARLEY SOUP FOR YOU AND YOUR DOG

This classic combination of chicken and pearl barley is the base for a tasty homemade soup that is just as healthy and yummy for you as it is for your dog. It comes together quickly and easily from a whole chicken carcass and orange vegetables – like in the old days when people used bones instead of just throwing them away.

Ingredients:
· roasted chicken carcass
· 2 garlic cloves, peeled
· 7 cups of water
· 1 cup carrots
· 2 apples
· 1 pound sweet potatoes
· ½ cup pearl barley
· 1 ½ tsp ground flaxseed

Preparation:
Put the chicken carcass and the garlic cloves in a large pot with seven cups of water. Bring to a boil, reduce heat, and simmer for about one hour.
In the meantime, peel the carrots and apples and cut into pieces. Wash or peel the sweet potatoes and chop roughly.

Run the chicken broth mixture through a sieve into a clean pot. Remove any remaining meat from the chicken bones and reserve on a separate plate. Add the vegetables, apples and pearl barley to the broth. Cover, bring to a boil, reduce heat, and simmer for about one hour.

Using an immersion blender or food processor, puree the vegetables in the soup. Add the reserved chicken meat, garnish with the flaxseed, and serve.

58

WORK OUT WITH YOUR DOG/DOG WALK FITNESS

Kill two birds with one stone – do Dog Walk Fitness for some of your workouts!

Jogging alone really isn't enough for the two of you – you want to use more muscle groups. Before you attempt this with your dog, it's important that he has reached his adult size and is healthy, and has mastered all basic commands if at all possible.

Okay, let's get started with our endurance interval training – an excellent workout for your heart and circulatory system.

If you want to do this workout on leash, I recommend putting a harness on your dog.

1. Start with a warm-up: five minutes of normal walking so that you and your dog can get limber.

2. Then, increase your pace (walking or jogging) and make sure your dog does the same. After five minutes at this faster pace, you can slow down again.

3. For the next five minutes, your dog has a "free" period and can sniff, dawdle, and determine his pace himself – and you must go as slowly or as quickly as necessary to enable him to do that.

4. Then, switch back to a medium walk or jog and hold that pace for ten minutes, keeping your breathing steady during that time. Your dog stays at your side.

5. Switch back to your normal walking pace, relax your body, and praise your dog. After five minutes, start your next training interval.

Over time, you can extend the duration of this workout, because this is, after all, endurance training. But remember to give your dog regular sniff-and-dawdle breaks, because endless running is boring for him – and you should both get something out of your workouts.
Once you have built up your fitness and are ready for a challenge, you can start adding push-ups to your endurance training – together!

TEAM PUSH-UPS

First, you have to teach your dog to place his front paws against a tree on command. Once you have that down, you can begin with tree-based push-ups.

1. Go into push-up position against a tree trunk and give your dog the command to put his front paws on the tree trunk ("On the tree!" or "Tree!"). Bend your elbows and tighten your stomach. Make sure that your body remains flat as a board. Press away from the tree trunk and give your dog the command to do the same (e.g., "And away!")

2. Take two minutes to do two to four push-ups on the tree while your dog also puts his paws on the tree and pushes himself away two to four times.

3. Praise your athletic dog and continue your walk until you see another inviting tree, tree stump, or fallen tree. This time, take three to four minutes and do four to eight push-ups on the tree. Your dog can press himself away from the tree four to eight times as well.

4. Praise your dog while you shake out your arms and legs. Continue your walk with pride, with your head held high!

59

TELL YOUR DOG A STORY

After a long, hard day, sit down with your dog and tell him a story. Use lots of words that he knows, like his name and the words *"squirrel"* or *"bunny"*. It's also important to include the word *"treat"* or *"cookie."*
Tell him how much you need him.
That's something you can never hear too often.

60

"GO TO BED"

High-energy dogs usually love doing tricks and are born circus clowns. (This generally does not apply to Great Pyrenees, Newfoundlands, or Galgos. Such antics are beneath their dignity.)

The trick I'm about to describe to you used to be known as "Bang!" But nowadays, it's somehow depressing to shoot your own dog, even if it's just with a finger. "Going to bed" is so much more peaceful and useful.

And it's also a command that you can build incidentally: every time you see your dog lying peacefully on his side, tell him "Go to bed!" and quietly praise him (maybe just stroke him from neck to tail in large movements so you don't accidentally make him jump to his feet).

After a few days of practice, tell your dog "Down!", kneel down next to him, and gently roll him onto his side. Praise him. Tell him "Go to bed" and repeat these steps over the next few days.

Then start by first saying "Go to bed" and giving a hand signal for him to lay down. When he complies, repeat "Go to bed" and gently roll him onto his side. If you use a clicker with your dog, click each individual step. Please be very sparing with the cookies you give to your dog while he is lying down!

Then add a hand signal for "Go to bed": Press your palms together and lean the side of your head on them as if you are placing your head on a pillow.

Once your dog understands what you're asking, stand up (use an open palm held toward him like a stop sign to tell him "Stay!"). If he knows the "Stay!" command, even better. Have him lie there for only a few seconds and then release him by saying "Time to get up!" Then praise him very, very enthusiastically!

Practice this trick once a day for a week (neither you nor your dog should be sick of the trick before he has even mastered it). Gradually increase the time your dog is "in bed" up to about a minute.

Start giving the command from a standing position. If you need to, bend down to "help" your dog lay down, but then stand up straight again, wait for a bit, and then let him get up again. The whole process may take a week or two, but before you know it, your dog will "go to bed" at the mildest command from you.

61

BREAK UP WITH YOUR BOYFRIEND OR GIRLFRIEND IF HE/SHE DOESN'T LIKE YOUR DOG

I am totally serious here: it might sound harsh, especially because deep down in your heart of hearts, you're secretly convinced you'll never find anyone better – but if your partner doesn't like something that is essential to your life and is not willing to make a compromise for you, then the two of you are simply not compatible. For me personally, for example, a barely acceptable compromise would be for me to have only two dogs instead of the eight I currently have. If your boyfriend or girlfriend were obsessed with mountain biking, would you even dream of making him or her choose between you and a bicycle? Not a chance. And if the issue is a dog you already have, it would be the height of heartlessness to condemn him to losing his home merely because someone thinks he's annoying, big, too hairy, or too whatever. As a warning, buy yourself a T-shirt that says "I only come with dogs." That should make any potential mates think twice.

62

TRAVEL COMPANION

Particularly with a dog who has trouble bonding to you, or two dogs who can't seem to get along well with each other, going on a trip together is very beneficial. If you haven't already read John Steinbeck's "Travels with Charley" on this subject, you should – it spawned the entire dog travel genre. Take a trip by car, drive to the most beautiful areas of forest and fields, take long walks, sit by a lake or at the top of a hill and talk to your dog(s) – and to your human companions too, if any are with you. But also spend a lot of time in silence, read, just think about whatever is on your mind. Look at picturesque cities and colorful markets, and sleep in small inns that allow dogs! Plan your route in advance so you know whether and where you can bring your dog(s) along. Otherwise, you might find yourself unexpectedly sleeping in your car. Although – that can also be a great bonding moment, too. The only problem is that you might not sleep very well because as a human, it's really hard to roll up into a ball on a car seat. Look at old castles, visit farm parks and show your dog animals he's never seen before: pigs, goats, cows, and/or horses. Just make sure that he doesn't bark at them or chase them. That makes you and your dog rather less popular – with both the animals and their owners!

Follow your heart and your map, and observe how your dog reacts to everything he's experiencing. This will help you get to know yourself and your dog(s) all over again.

63

A BUILD-IT-YOURSELF BOTTLE GAME FOR DOGS

Agility or "intelligence" games for dogs require patience and some dexterity from your dog – and when you make them yourself, they demand the same qualities from the owner. But you'll both beam with pride when you have completed the process!

You'll need:
- · 1 rectangular piece of wood (for the base)
- · 2 rectangular or round wooden supports
- · 1 round wooden or aluminum rod
- · 1 to 4 plastic two-liter bottles
- · 2 to 4 wood screws (or dowels)
- · glue
- · screwdriver or electric screwdriver
- · power drill with auger

Instructions:

1. Drill a hole in the side of each of your vertical supports near the top. Measure carefully: the holes must be at precisely the same height. Your holes have to be large enough for the wooden or aluminum rod to fit through and turn.

2. Cut two parallel holes in the upper third of the plastic bottle(s). (Same diameter as for the supports.)

3. Use screws and glue to join the two vertical supports to the base along the long outside edges (for large or clumsy dogs, use dowels for greater stability). If using glue, let it dry for 24 hours.

4. Run the rod through the first vertical support, through the bottle(s), and then through the second vertical support.

5. Put treats or dry kibble inside the bottle(s).

Tip: To keep your dog busy longer, or for multi-dog use, you can use a longer rod and attach several bottles.

64

THANK YOUR DOG FOR ETERNAL LIFE …

… although you should always be extremely leery of any treatment that claims to stop, ease, or even heal several very different illnesses. As a rule, "miracles" like that tend to help only the "miracle healers." But here is the exception to the rule: a single remedy can help against everything from heart and circulatory disease, cancer, and back pain to osteoporosis, depression, and many other maladies as well. In addition, if used properly, it has nearly no side effects and doesn't cost you anything but time.

Its name is: walking. The effect is measurable and increases at higher doses. It is proven effective! Walking helps cure so many medical problems. Really!

Regular walking (five times a week for only 30 minutes each time)
· Strengthens the immune system
· Reduces the risk of glaucoma
· Stimulates the release of endorphins
· Relieves stress and fatigue after just ten minutes
· Cuts Alzheimer's risk in half
· Improves heart health and relieves high blood pressure
· Reduces the risk of diabetes
· Strengthens muscles and increases the load-bearing capacity of joints
· Relieves joint and back pain
· Reduces loss of bone density, which reduces the risk of osteoporosis

· Trains your sense of balance
· Relieves depression and reduces panic attacks
· Reduces the risk of many types of cancer
· Increases your metabolic rate

As a dog owner, you go out and walk at least twice a day for 30 minutes each day. You can't get any closer to immortality than that.

65

JUST BE TOGETHER AND DO NOTHING FOR A CHANGE

Our dogs can no longer decide for themselves how much exercise and work they need and want every day. So most of us have a permanent guilty conscience when it comes to our dogs – because we always have the feeling that they are somehow getting shortchanged. To make up for the fact that we don't have a farm with dozens of animals and jobs available, we tend to overdo it when planning how we will exercise and occupy them. And then we're surprised if a dog is still edgy, "amped up," and generally restless.

If you take a closer look, you suddenly see that the dog in question has a daily routine that makes an ambitious private school student's day look like a cakewalk.

Dogs don't need to be entertained every minute of the day. Not even working dogs actually work all day. A guard dog ambles away the day on his property and only very rarely has to deal with an intruder. A professional sheepdog usually works no more than two hours a day: a herd is normally only driven for short distances, and even that is not a daily occurrence. Hunting dogs work mostly in the fall. During the rest of the year, they accompany their master across his territory and watch him perform minor tasks like repairing fences and checking tree stands. Even sled dogs only have a four-month season – they are kept in large enclosures and allowed to take it easy the rest of the year.

Don't confuse the rituals that you have put together for your dog with his actual needs. Try not doing anything with him for a whole day besides just hanging out together, without pushing him aside as a minor detail. For most dogs, the thing they care about most is being with you. That's it.

66

A SCAVENGER HUNT FOR YOUR DOG AND HIS (AND YOUR!) FRIENDS

Some things are just more fun with others, or can only be done with a group. Do the words "scavenger hunt" ring a bell? It's a game played outdoors where two teams face off against each other and follow clues that have been laid out in advance. You have to perform certain tasks at specific points in order to get to the finish line. For example, you might have to figure out where a "treasure" or reward is hidden – or just where the path continues. The organizers put each "mission" in a small tin can at points they mark on a map. Depending on how long the course is, one or more helpers may be stationed along the way in case someone gets hurt, lost, or needs a clue. This game can be adapted to work wonderfully with dogs as well.

Try the following ideas for a great scavenger hunt with human-canine teams:
· The dogs have to jump over some barriers, fetch something, and then jump back over the barriers to bring the item back to their human team-mates. Dogs get points for each jump they successfully complete and for the retrieve.

· Dogs have to run a certain distance (maybe ten yards) without eating treats to the left and right of the path. Only after they cross the finish line can their people give them a few as a reward.

· Dog puzzle (for people): Type up a list of dog breeds and print it out. Cut each breed name after every third letter, mix up the resulting small pieces, and have people put the names of the dog breeds back together.

· Quiz with multiple choice questions about dogs and/or dog care and training.

67

TAKE EXTRA GOOD CARE OF YOUR SENIOR DOG

Even if your dog will always be an adorable fluffy puppy in your eyes, there is a point past which you cannot deny that he has become an old man (or woman). This is largely dependent on your dog's breed: small dogs aren't in their "golden years" until they are ten or twelve years old, while very large dogs like Great Danes, Irish Wolfhounds, or Leonbergers are already part of the "old guard" at seven or eight. And of course, just as with humans, genetics play a role in the aging process, along with nutrition, the environment, and the stress the dog was subjected to over the course of his life.

The right combination of good preventive care and careful observation can add years to your best friend's life.

PAY CLOSE ATTENTION TO HIS TEETH

Oral hygiene in particular cannot be neglected as your dog gets older. If your dog has bad breath, it is usually due to an infected tooth or bacteria in the periodontal pockets. Regular brushing with a soft child-size toothbrush and regular dental checks at the vet can prevent an infection from taking root and possibly even damaging other organs of the body.

ADJUST HOW MUCH AND WHAT YOU FEED AS THE DOG AGES

Most older dogs need the same nutrients, but fewer calories than young dogs. Their metabolism slows because they are no longer leaping around like a Rockette, they are doing less mental work, and they often don't do as many long and crazy walks due to arthritis. Your dog still wants high-quality nutrition, but raw food should no longer be on the menu (cooked food is somewhat predigested and therefore easier on his stomach). He needs additional omega-3 fatty acids to fight infection and arthritis, and he may need collagen-containing supplements for his joints.

GO TO THE VET MORE OFTEN

If your dog has been very healthy throughout his life, you may not notice right away that he is moving more slowly, or doesn't see or hear as well. Go see a vet at least twice a year. It may be a good idea to do regular blood work to discover lurking infections immediately before they become a real problem.

MAKE YOUR HOME SENIOR-FRIENDLY

In the same way you once "puppy-proofed" your house many years ago, you can now make your house a bit more senior-friendly. If your dog has hip dysplasia or arthritis, get a ramp to help him get into the car or onto your sofa. If he doesn't see as well as before, make sure it's easy for him to get to his food and water bowls. If you have any extremely slippery flooring in your house, think about putting a rug over it to keep your dog from slipping or having to walk with enormous care to cross it. Make sure he has a comfy dog bed that is the right size to keep his bones from aching. If you have rambunctious children, make sure they leave your dog in peace. And make sure your dog gets enough sleep without excluding him from family life.

BE ON THE LOOKOUT FOR CHANGES

Watch him and see if he walks differently than he used to, whether he might have a slight limp, or if any lumps or bumps develop on his body. Observe his appetite and weight. Is he drinking too little or too much? How does his skin feel? If you notice any changes, report them to your veterinarian.

It might be a little more work than you're used to compared to his younger days – but that's part of taking responsibility for another living being. Your dog has been at your side and cared for you through good times and bad – so now it's time for you to return the favor.

68

LIVERWURST TEA

A drink worthy of royalty: what a wonderful, creamy cup of cocoa is to humans, that is what liverwurst tea is to dogs.

When you come home from a long, very wet, or bitterly cold walk, or when your dog needs some comfort or isn't drinking enough, dissolve a tablespoon of liverwurst in hot water. Once the heavenly mixture has cooled off to a drinkable temperature, give it to your dog.

Another tip: Liverwurst tea is also a great "sauce" to put on the food of picky eaters.

69

SHARE A SMOOTHIE WITH YOUR DOG

Smoothies are a phenomenal way to get your fruits and veggies in a quick, delicious package! And just like you make smoothies for yourself, you can make one for your dog!

There are a million variations on the tasty liquid breakfast treat. You can toss pretty much anything you like to eat in a blender. As long as you stay away from cocoa powder, vanilla ice cream, and similar items, it's only healthy (and fair!) to give your dog half.

BREAKFAST SMOOTHIE

Oats are a complete source of amino acids, contain potassium and folate, and are high in fiber. Almonds are rich in unsaturated fats. Maple syrup is high in zinc, which is an antioxidant that slows arteriosclerosis.

· 1 cup strawberries (fresh or frozen)
· ½ of a medium banana
· ⅓ cup low-fat yogurt
· ¼ cup ground almonds
· ½ cup rolled oats
· 1 tsp maple syrup

Put all ingredients in a blender and mix for 40 seconds at the highest speed. Done!

GREEN SMOOTHIE

Cucumbers have lots of vitamin C, vitamin A, folate, manganese, silicon, potassium, and magnesium.

· 1 organic cucumber (Conventional cucumbers are heavily waxed, and the peel may contain high levels of pesticides. There are also a lot of nutrients in the peel, so be sure to get an organic one.)
· ½ of a honeydew, or 2 pears
· 2 tbsp fresh mint
· ½ cup water
· 2 cups baby spinach

Put all ingredients in the blender and mix for 30 seconds at the highest speed. Bon appétit!

70

MAKE A SCENT PILLOW FOR YOUR DOG

Essential oils have been used on people and animals for thousands of years to enhance mood and support physical and mental well-being. You can rub them in, inhale them, or take them as a pill. Dogs are extremely smell-oriented; the many, many hair follicles in their skin are ideal for the absorption of lipophilic substances like essential oils or fatty plant-based oils.

Essential oils are ephemeral components of therapeutically effective plants. They have demonstrable effects depending on which plant or plant part they are extracted from. Essential oils can work via the skin, the mucosa, or the nasal passages.

The following items may NOT be used on dogs: nature-identical or synthetic scented oils like the cheap ones you get at the drugstore, standardized or rectified essential oils, mineral oils, refined oils as carrier substances, scented candles or other sprays. Dog perfumes and synthetically scented

dog shampoo are the precise opposite of aromatherapy – they disturb the sensitive canine nose a great deal and can also trigger allergic skin reactions.

Aromatherapy on dogs has also proven very helpful for
· calming fearful or aggressive dogs
· general stimulation or relaxation
· boosting appetite

Although in theory any scents can be used with dogs, you should check and see which fragrances your dog likes or dislikes. And remember the basic rule for any use of essential oils: less is more!

Effects of essential oils
· **Lavender** is calming
· **Lemon balm** is calming and promotes harmony
· **Baldrian** is calming and promotes sleep
· **Lemon** is stimulating (always dilute it!)
· **Anise** stimulates the appetite
· **Chamomile** is relaxing
· **Peppermint** counters nausea and vomiting (very good for dogs with motion sickness)
· **Rose** or **neroli**: eases sadness and feelings of loss

- **Eucalyptus** or **myrtle**: effective against colds and respiratory illnesses
- **German (blue) chamomile** and/or **helichrysum**: for wounds; also a strong calming agent
- **Rose geranium**: eases fatigue and exhaustion and helps relieve skin problems

The best way to begin is to place a scented pillow or small cloth on or against his bed. Put one drop of the oil you have selected on the pillow and put it wherever your dog spends the most time. If your dog doesn't lie down there anymore, he doesn't like the scent you chose – just remove the scented pillow. Once you have figured out which oils (or mixtures) your dog likes best, you can also use an oil burner or diffuser to spread the scent throughout the room.

71

PLANT A FRUIT CRATE WITH GRASS

Dogs like to eat grass. Contrary to the old folk sayings, it has nothing to do with rain coming soon or a change in the weather. Eating grass is to dogs what eating a salad is to us. It gives them some fiber and even seems to have a social component: if you run into me and my eight dogs out in the meadow one morning and see them all standing around, happily munching on the long grass, it looks like I'm taking my herd out to graze. When dogs have stomachaches or feel nauseous, they eat grass to help them throw up. This is completely normal and helps them empty their stomachs, which in turn helps them rid their bodies of any indigestible foreign objects.

In most parks, the grass is usually cut very short and/or peed on by other dogs, so it is no longer suitable for eating. So do your dog a favor and give him the gift of his very own bed of long grass. Don't let it get taller than about eight inches, or your dog will no longer find it tasty. If you "only" have a balcony, or not even that, take an empty fruit crate, line the bottom and sides with plastic, fill it with dirt, and plant grass seeds in it. Once the grass is six to eight inches tall, you can serve it to your dog. A tip from my own personal experience: it's best if you put the crate in your kitchen somewhere where you're not constantly tripping over it.

72

GO FOR A WALK IN THE HOURS BEFORE DAWN

Okay, I admit this isn't a good idea if you live in a bad neighborhood or in Florida, where you might encounter alligators at night. But otherwise, a "proper" summery walk as night fades and morning mist rises is a fantastic way to freshen up a bond that may have become a little neglected. However, you should not have a dog that barks his head off at the sight of a field mouse, or your fun might be severely curtailed. Get a flashlight, a sweater, rubber boots, and your dog on a six-foot leash and take off – preferably in an area you know well to reduce the risk of getting lost in the twilight. This is a bit of an adventure.

In a normal forest or meadow, there's really nothing that can befall you during that false dawn around five in the morning that couldn't happen just as easily at five in the afternoon – and you have your dog to protect you to boot. You will, however, hear a lot more than during normal daylight hours: many, many animals are active at night. You'll hear (or maybe even see) martens and weasels as well as deer and foxes, and if you're extremely lucky, you might even see one of the larger owl species once your eyes have adjusted to the dark.

Listen and try to determine the order in which the birds wake up: the avian concert goes full blast once the sun rises. Each bird species waits for a specific amount of light before it starts singing. Usually only the males sing. First you'll hear the black redstart, then blackbirds, robins, chickadees. Then the cuckoo chimes in, the wren, the chaffinch, the nondescript chiff-chaff, the serin, the starling, and finally the white wagtail. I have to admit: those are the birds in my region. Find out about "yours". In late summer everywhere, the forest actually grows quiet because most birds are molting and stubbornly silent.

These are the amazing things that people see, hear, and think at this early hour of the morning. The air smells of dried hay, of ash trees, and clouds of fox pee. Veils of moisture rise from the dewy meadow full of pink ragged-robin.

If this is how you start your morning, you will be unstoppable for the rest of the day. I promise.

73

GO TO A MAJOR DOG SHOW WITH YOUR DOG

Dog shows are their own planet, with their own terminology, their own rules and sounds, and their own unique odor (a mix of pig's ears, wet dogs, kibble, human sweat and convention center carpet), the combination of which can overwhelm your senses. For some people, dog shows become a way of life: every weekend, they drive their RV from one show site to the next, know all of the judges by name and certainly know all of the other dogs, and like overeager tennis parents, they pit their dog against carefully selected competition over and over.

That might sound like more of a deterrent – but it is still a very interesting experience to visit one of the major dog shows at least once. You get to see the loveliest (or supposedly loveliest) examples of up to 140 breeds. You'll see plus-size people galloping through the ring next to their elegant greyhounds trotting nonchalantly along. You will be amazed at the glorious coats of dogs that were originally bred to point feathered game in wet underbrush, dogs that now only get to walk on asphalt in full-body coats or at least leggings, so their precious hair won't break. You'll see tough-as-nails terriers who couldn't care less about trophies and ribbons and leave no doubt that they are still lightning-fast ratters outside the show ring. You'll stroll past dogs that lie on their grooming tables with the grace and ease of a Claudia Schiffer, dogs that simply look right through admirers. You can make a great study of the similarities between master and dog that are more readily on display here than anywhere else, here in this bizarre dog show world. If you don't believe me, go to the Briard ring and study the owners carefully. Then do the same with the Weimaraners and the Golden Retrievers ...

And then, buy your dog a huge bag of dried cow's ears and assure him that if there were a contest for the best personality, he would win it in a landslide.

DOGS LOVE THEIR OWN BREED

If you are the owner of a purebred, a trip to a breed club meeting will also be a treat for your dog. Most purebred dogs are a bit prejudiced, true, but it's not political at all. It has something to do with their formative experiences during their first few weeks of life: they jump for joy when they see other dogs of their own breed because their mother's mug and faces of possible relatives were what they saw the most.

Pugs, for example, can hardly contain themselves when they meet other pugs, and greyhounds seem most content when they can run and/or lie around with others of their own kind. Do your dog a favor and bring him to his own sort of family reunion, whether it's a meeting at your breeder's or a walk sponsored by your local breed club. You'll see: your dog will feel like a king.

74

LAY DOWN A TRAIL

Your dog's nose is a high-performance instrument. He has about 200 million olfactory receptors, while people only have a pathetic five million. Harness your dog's olfactory superpowers and lay down a scent trail for him.

For your first try, use food with a strong odor like sausage or smelly cheese. Put the bait in an old sock or stocking and tie the top in a knot. Now, drag the stinky stocking behind you through your yard, a meadow, or an (empty!) parking lot – choose a place with as few distractions as possible. At the end of the trail, place the filled stocking in the immediate vicinity. Now go get your dog and put a harness on him if possible so he can track the scent (or "scent the trail" as people say about tracking dogs) to his heart's content. It's best if you show him the beginning of the trail you've laid (if you have a terrible memory, mark the spot beforehand) and command him to "Track it!" to follow the trail. When he finds the stocking, reward your dog with the food inside!

The better your dog gets at this game, the less smelly the contents of the stocking need to be – this increases the challenge.

75

WALKING IN THE SNOW

Dog walks have a dark side, which you usually see very late at night in November or in the snow when you reeeeaally don't want to go out with the dog one more time. We've all been there: you were at a really great party, you're tired from all the talking and drinking, your house is warm and cozy, and your bed seems like the most alluring place on Earth ...
No matter. The dog needs to go out again. And then he'll let you sleep in longer in the morning. Softly cursing, you pull on boots, coat, scarf, and hat and stomp out into the night, which is the polar opposite of mild.

Maybe it's snowing, too, really big flakes that cover everything – branches, the curvy silhouettes of cars, rooftops, fences and trash cans. While you blaze a trail in the snow with your feet, you see how the snow piles up on your dog's back.

The windows in the houses and apartments are all dark. Your virtuous neighbors all went to bed long ago, except for one window on the top floor where the blue light of a television is flickering. Not a single car has disturbed the new-fallen snow on the street. By morning, the soft whiteness will have been swept, plowed, cleared, shoved into piles, salted, melted, and trampled on. But for now, the snow is lying pure and innocent on the streets.

Without your dog, you wouldn't have gotten to experience this sight; you wouldn't have noticed how invigorating the cold air is. And suddenly you're wide awake and oddly full of energy. The streetlights show you which direction the flakes are falling from the sky. The low clouds reflect the lights of the city, which makes the sky look unnaturally bright.

Let your dog off leash. Make a few snowballs and throw them to your dog. Watch how he runs through the snow – now he doesn't need a ball, snowball or frisbee to run. He runs simply because the snow invites him to. When our dogs run all out over a big open stretch, our hearts open wide, and maybe we run part of the way with them.

By the time you get back home, you've remembered the magic of dog walks: how something that you really, *really* didn't want to do and were basically *forced* to do turned into something you are suddenly pretty thankful for.

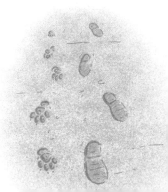

76

GRAIN-FREE CHRISTMAS LIVER BISCOTTI

Are you still looking for a Christmas present for your dog or for friends with dogs? This recipe will guarantee you the undying devotion of every dog in your neighborhood. Buy a cute tin to put the treats in, tie a pretty bow around it, and voilà, your own personal Christmas present is ready!

Ingredients:
· 1 pound beef liver
· 2 eggs
· 1 ⅓ cups chickpea flour
· ⅔ cup grated Appenzeller or cheddar cheese

Preparation:
Preheat oven to 300°F.

Puree the liver and eggs in a food processor, or use an immersion blender. Combine the mixture with the chickpea flour in a large bowl and stir in the grated cheese. Spread the resulting dough onto a parchment paper-lined baking sheet. Bake for 25 minutes.

Remove the baking sheet from the oven. Once it has cooled, flip the treats over and remove the parchment paper.

Cut the treats into biscotti-sized pieces and place them on another parchment paper-lined baking sheet. Dry them out for three hours in a 300°F oven until they have become very dry, crunchy cookies.

77

EMBARKING ON THE FINAL ADVENTURE

Thankfully, most of the time, it only slowly becomes apparent that it is time to let your dog go, but it still usually catches you flat-footed. No matter how much time you've had to prepare, no matter how many dogs you've had to say good-bye to before, it always comes too soon.

If it is at all possible, say farewell to your dog. Spend your last hours with him in such a way that he thinks he's already in doggie paradise. Have a breakfast of croissants and hot dogs, sit with him somewhere he's always liked to sit, pet him and tell him what a wonderful dog he is, all the wonderful things you've learned from him, and how great it was to have him by your side for so many years. If you have other pets, make sure they can say good-bye as well (they know what's happening, I assure you). If he can't walk anymore, sit down next to his bed, pet him, and make the farewell easy on him. You're allowed to cry, but don't come completely unglued: it would create tremendous conflict in your dog, because he is hardly in a position to comfort you and he may not feel comfortable enough to let go if he sees you in such a state.

If at all possible, have him euthanized at home in his familiar environment, with all of the smells he knows. Stay right there with him.

You had — no matter how long or not-long-enough you had — a terrific life together. He showed you things that no one else was ever aware of before, and he had quirks and oddities and foibles like no one before him. He helped you grow beyond yourself at certain times, and he always made you laugh, day in and day out. He was there when no one else was, and he was always, always certain that whatever you just said was brilliant. He rarely questioned your meal planning, and he thought you were gorgeous, regardless of whether you'd showered or put on a presentable outfit. He accepted you as you truly are and asked no questions.

You protected his life and accepted him the way he was – you may have adjusted him a little or taught him a few manners, but he showed you that you have to accept personalities for what they are. It is what it is.

You won't get any closer to Buddhism in this life.

He was your friend in good times as well as bad, just as you were for him. It is unspeakably sad that he has to go now – but it was wonderful that you had the privilege of having such a true and wondrous friend.

How lucky the two of you were to have this life together.

BIOGRAPHY

Katharina von der Leyen is a journalist and book author and is one of the best-known writers on dogs. She has published numerous guides, novels, columns, and magazine articles about dogs and living with them in outlets including *Dogs, Myself,* the *Frankfurter Allgemeine Sonntagszeitung, Welt am Sonntag, Bild am Sonntag,* and many more. She is a top-drawer dog blogger with her successful *blog www.lumpi4.de.* She has about eight dogs herself and has never met a dog she didn't like.

You still can't get enough of dogs?

KATHARINA VON DER LEYEN
FOR THE LOVE OF DOGS

Dogs aren't exactly shy when it comes to expressing their feelings. They do everything we humans are afraid to: dogs are ecstatic and boisterous, tactless, openly enthusiastic, take delight in rolling in disgusting things, sleep when they're tired, and don't care if you snore. Dogs teach us that joy is a way of life and that it does not depend on what happens each day; they always assume something fabulous is going to happen today.
This book shows dogs as they truly are – bursting with happiness, tired after a hard play session, chewing on a $300 running shoe, and locked in battle with a roll of toilet paper. It shows puppies so worn out by life's thrills that they fall asleep precisely where they were just standing on their wobbly little legs, and it shows dogs getting slower, older, and wiser, with a gaze that will break your heart.

ISNB: 978-3832732912
35.00 USD

teNeues

Katharina von der Leyen

F O R T H E L O V E O F

Dogs

IMPRINT

© 2017 teNeues Media GmbH & Co. KG, Kempen
All rights reserved.

Editorial coordination by Stephanie Bräuer
Translation by Amanda Ennis (in memory of Tika)
Illustrations: Elke Reinhart
Creative Director: Martin Graf
Design & Layout: Vero Holubovsky
Production: Dieter Haberzettl

Published by teNeues Publishing Group

teNeues Media GmbH & Co. KG
Am Selder 37, 47906 Kempen, Germany
Phone: +49-(0)2152-916-0
Fax: +49-(0)2152-916-111
e-mail: books@teneues.com

Munich Office
Pilotystraße 4, 80538 Munich, Germany
Phone: +49-(0)89-443-8889-62
e-mail: bkellner@teneues.com

Press department: Andrea Rehn
Phone: +49-(0)2152-916-202
e-mail: arehn@teneues.com

www.teneues.com

ISBN 978-3-96171-059-1

Library of Congress Number: 2017941972

Printed in the Czech Republic

teNeues Publishing Company
7 West 18th Street, New York, NY 10011, USA
Phone: +1-212-627-9090
Fax: +1-212-627-9511

teNeues Publishing UK Ltd.
2 Ferndene Road, London SE24 0AQ, UK
Phone: +44-(0)20-3542-8997

teNeues France S.A.R.L.
39, rue des Billets, 18250 Henrichemont, France
Phone: +33-(0)2-4826-9348
Fax: +33-(0)1-7072-3482

MIX
Papier aus verantwortungsvollen Quellen
Paper from responsible sources
FSC
www.fsc.org
FSC® C005833

teNeues Publishing Group
Kempen
Berlin
London
Munich
New York
Paris

teNeues